LITTLE PRETTY AND THE EXCEPTIONAL

ALSO BY ANUSREE ROY

Pyaasa & Letters to My Grandma
Brothel #9
Sultans of the Street

LITTLE PRETTY AND THE EXCEPTIONAL

ANUSREE ROY

PLAYWRIGHTS CANADA PRESS
TORONTO

First edition: February 2025
Printed and bound in Canada by Imprimerie Gauvin Ltée, Gatineau

Jacket art and design by Christine Mangosing
Author photo by Ian Brown

Playwrights Canada Press
202-269 Richmond St. W., Toronto, ON M5V 1X1
416.703.0013 | info@playwrightscanada.com | www.playwrightscanada.com

For professional or amateur production rights, please contact:
Ian Arnold, Catalyst TCM
PO Box 98074 RPO Queen and Carlaw Toronto, ON M4M 3L9
416-568-8673 | ian@catalysttcm.com

LIBRARY AND ARCHIVES CANADA CATALOGUING IN PUBLICATION
Title: Little pretty and the exceptional / Anusree Roy.
Names: Roy, Anusree, author.
Description: First edition. | In English, with some text in Panjabi with English translation.
Identifiers: Canadiana (print) 20240528352 | Canadiana (ebook) 20240529812 | ISBN 9780369105363 (softcover) | ISBN 9780369105370 (PDF) | ISBN 9780369105387 (EPUB)
Subjects: LCGFT: Drama.
Classification: LCC PS8635.O898 L58 2025 | DDC C812/.6—dc23

Playwrights Canada Press staff work across Turtle Island, on Treaty 7, Treaty 13, and Treaty 20 territories, which are the current and ancestral homes of the Anishinaabe Nations (Ojibwe / Chippewa, Odawa, Potawatomi, Algonquin, Saulteaux, Nipissing, and Mississauga / Michi Saagiig), the Blackfoot Confederacy (Kainai, Piikani, and Siksika), néhiyaw, Sioux, Stoney Nakoda, Tsuut'ina, Wendat, and members of the Haudenosaunee Confederacy (Mohawk, Oneida, Onondaga, Cayuga, Seneca, and Tuscarora), as well as Metis and Inuit peoples. It always was and always will be Indigenous land.

We acknowledge the financial support of the Canada Council for the Arts, the Ontario Arts Council (OAC), Ontario Creates, the Government of Ontario, and the Government of Canada for our publishing activities.

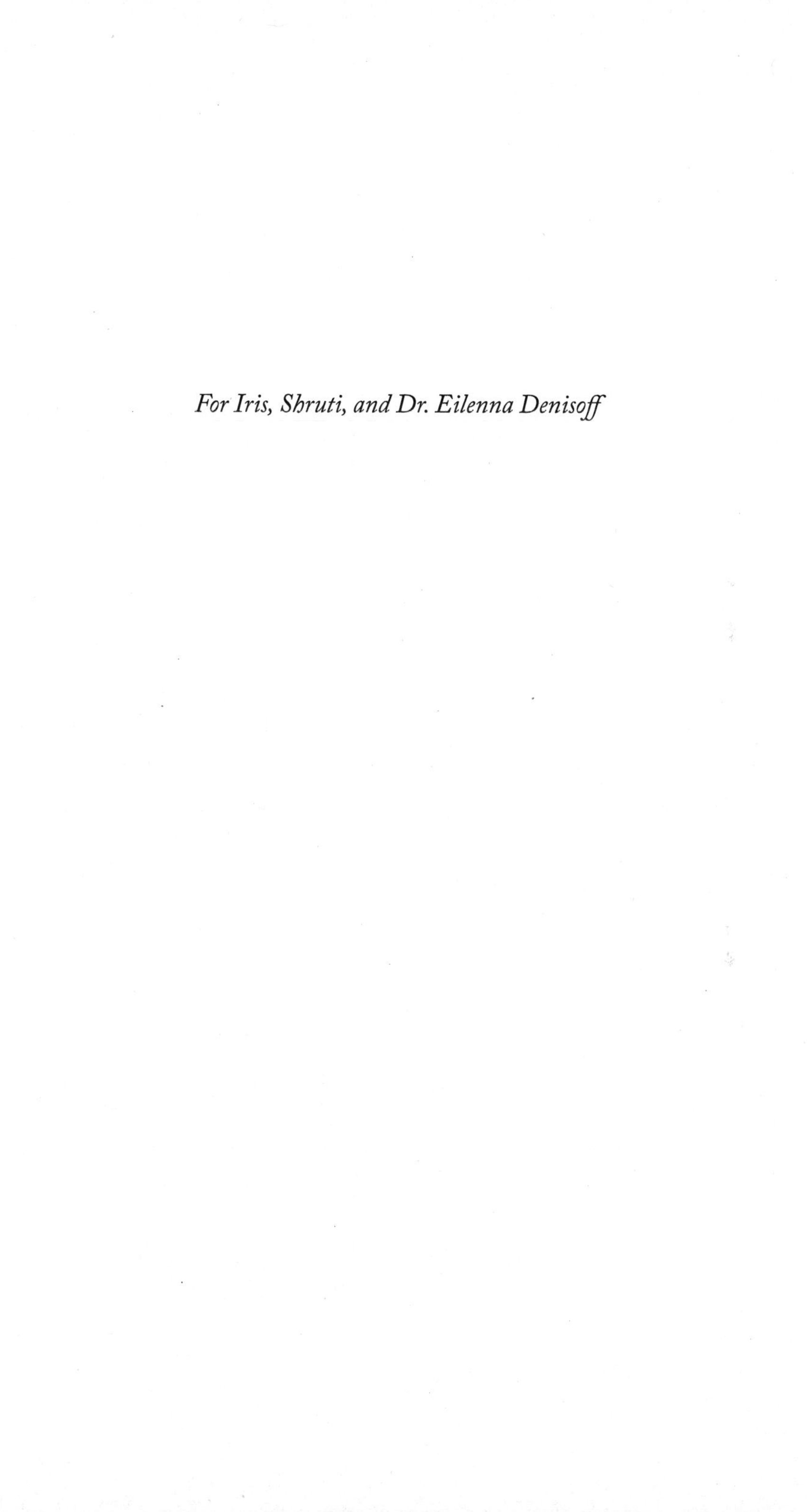

For Iris, Shruti, and Dr. Eilenna Denisoff

IT'S TIME TO TALK ABOUT MENTAL HEALTH

BY ANUSREE ROY, AS TOLD TO MAIJA KAPPLER

Little Pretty and The Exceptional is a play set in Toronto that examines the life of a father and his two daughters. As the play unfolds, we realize that one of them is in the depths of a mental health crisis. It's not a play *about* schizophrenia, because that's ineffective to me. It's about the human element. What is schizophrenia to a family? Who are we in troubling circumstances? Who do we become when we are faced with things that are bigger than we can comprehend?

In 2012 I started preliminary research on mental health. A play was coming; I could feel it. Around that same time I myself got very sick. On my thirtieth birthday I couldn't get out of bed, lying there with excruciating pain running up my spine. I was taken to the hospital and was diagnosed with arthritis in my spinal cord, my knees, and my eyes. It's a degenerative-progressive disease for which I have to do an intense amount of maintenance. I had to reorganize my whole life. As I was on the medical table hearing this diagnosis, with my future flashing before my eyes, I didn't realize that my own brain was absorbing this as trauma.

Six months later I found myself at a psychiatrist's office in Toronto Western Hospital talking about my mental state. I thought I was going crazy. Something was wrong in my head and I wasn't sure why. I was not who I thought I was. I was outside of my own body. I had gone mad. I didn't know where anything was; I didn't know who I was; nothing was making sense. I was scared of hurting myself. Everything was falling apart.

I had a fish at the time, and I would grab the fishbowl and start pacing down Palmerston Boulevard. I would find myself—no slippers, in pyjamas, huge loose T-shirt—walking down Palmerston and College, just repeating my own name to myself. Repeating my mother's name, my father's name, where I lived, what I did, who I was. That I was an actress and a writer and this is what I did for a living.

When I looked in the mirror I literally couldn't recognize myself. I obsessed over it for a year and a half. It was terrifying. I had to hide all of the mirrors in my home. I would find the walls inside my apartment moving, which a logical brain knows never happens. Your walls don't move. But literally, *literally*, walls were moving towards me. I was standing outside of my body. I could see myself from above the ceiling. I was in a state of such pure shock.

As I'm telling you this, it makes no sense. I'm aware of that. If somebody who's mentally healthy hears what I'm saying, it makes no sense. If you say to somebody, "I am outside of my body watching myself," it makes no sense. But that's just the reality of the brain. I could actually zoom out of my body and watch itself. It's the most absurd experience.

I had post-traumatic stress disorder (PTSD). I remember thinking, "But this is for soldiers who kill people, who go to war. Regular actresses and writers with a health diagnosis just go about their life, they don't stand in front of a mirror questioning who they are. Other people get diagnosed with *fatal* things. What I have is very serious, but I'm not dying." I remember saying to myself repeatedly: Why? Why can't my brain just move on? But my brain froze. It got stuck in a place of extreme fear and extreme trauma and extreme panic.

Another reflex that I had—another symptom of panic and trauma—was extreme dislocation. I would not know where I was, and my brain would trigger vomit. I remember being at work and suddenly I had no idea where I was or who people around me were, and my mouth was full of vomit. So: What do you do with the vomit? Do you swallow it? Or do you stand up and spit it out? That was the biggest conundrum of my life that year. What would I do with the vomit?

I tried to get on a list for PTSD treatment with the Centre for Addiction and Mental Health. It was a six-month wait. I remember thinking, "What if I'm not alive in six months? I can't wait for free PTSD treatment." And, thankfully, God blessed me with this job, because my treatment was $10,000 by the end of it, which I paid on my own. Ten grand is a lot of money. How do you afford that? It's made harder by the fact that our business is not sitting around for people. You still have to go on: the show's gotta get made, I have to meet my deadlines. Plays have to get done, audition deadlines have to be met, rent has to be paid. If I didn't keep working, I couldn't afford to go to therapy. I had to keep working. So do you swallow it, or do you not swallow it? It sounds so ridiculous now when I say it, but it's true. It's absolutely true. What do you do?

I did seven months of the wrong kind of treatment until I ended up with something that worked. I ended up finding a really good PTSD therapist, a cognitive behavioural therapist who focuses on trauma. Cognitive behavioural therapy (CBT) is *the* best for PTSD and trauma-related injuries. It opens up your brain in a different way. And I slowly, slowly started to learn what PTSD actually means, and what trauma does to someone's brain.

I remember doing a contract at Factory Theatre, and during preshow I had to put my makeup on, but I literally did not recognize myself in the mirror. I was seeing my therapist at the time and we were trying all kinds of tactics for my brain to move forward from that thought that it got stuck in. I found this tiny shard of a mirror at the dollar store so I wouldn't have to stare at my face and engage in panicked behaviour. The other actor at the show asked, "Why are you using a mirror that is smaller than your thumb? You look absurd." And I remember thinking, "Do I tell him or do I not tell him? He's my co-lead. Is he going to trust that the hundred pages I have memorized will all be there?" I don't want people to think I am not capable. How do you know somebody's not thinking, "Shit, we shouldn't hire her. She used to have PTSD." Who wants to work with an actress or a writer who is not well? It's very easy to tell somebody I have arthritis in my spine. It gets you a lot of compassion. But how could I tell someone I have PTSD right now—I can't recognize my own face?

At the time I hadn't met my partner. My greatest love, my best friend, was my mother. What if I forget her? My brain got stuck in that thought, which produced extreme traumatic fear, which led me to want to go to my parents' house every night to make sure my mom was okay. Which makes no logical sense to me now with a healthy brain. But I would go. Every night at midnight I would walk down the street, in pyjamas and with a fishbowl, in extreme panic and fear. And when I started to seek treatment that was the first thing my therapist stopped. She said, "No, no. No one's going to their parents' house. Tell your brain you're going to forget your mom. Do it. Let's tell the brain you're going to forget her. See what that does." I said, "You cannot be serious." My brain couldn't comprehend it. I told her I had to go to my parents' house. And she said: "So what? You have to do everything you're thinking?"

One of the CBT exercises was walking the long circular hallway of her office building. She walked behind me and would repeat instructions, and I had to learn to hear them and not respond: "Jump. Swing your arms. Walk faster. Walk slower. Talk to me. Keep your mouth shut. Don't open your eyes. Close your mouth." I would finish that exercise, not doing anything she demanded, and she would ask, "So, do you have to do everything you hear? No. You don't have to do everything your mind is telling you, because your mind is stuck in panic."

I felt like I was acting that entire year and a half of my life while I was suffering. I was putting out a version of myself, and then a whole other thing was happening in my head. I think four people knew about my PTSD. Other people I ran into would never, ever, ever know. But in both theatre and TV I felt comfortable because it's what I knew to be home. But what was uncomfortable was the elephant inside the home, which I never invited in. The acting community was amazing: everybody knew about my physical health because many people saw me walking with a cane. People were compassionate. Many people had to help me, give me rides. But I couldn't tell anybody about my PTSD, because—what do you tell people? I'm walking the streets of Toronto with my fishbowl? I'm repeating my name for hours on end? Or the walls are closing in on me, or I vomit in my mouth and I'm not sure if I should swallow or spit it out?

There were many times I thought I just wouldn't get better. I really, honestly thought that was my life. But I did get better after that year and a half. I have moved on with my life, and I have a great partner whom I married, and all of those wonderful things. However, the weight of what I am and who I am is still informed by something I have never talked about publicly.

What's important to me, and what I want to achieve by talking about this, is for anyone who reads this and who is suffering to know that there's treatment. Your mental health is equally as important as your physical health. People who are struggling are not alone. You are not alone. Many people have done it. I'm a creature of loneliness, and I enjoy my own company. But the loneliness of the noise in your head is a very different loneliness.

Now that I've recovered and ten years have gone by, I still find myself hesitant. The first time I ever wrote about this was in the playwright's note for the *Little Pretty* program. But I've never, ever discussed it, because it's the most traumatic thing of my life, the most personal thing of my life. It's my greatest grief. The part of me that struggles thinks, "You're exposing your depths of despair. Will you still be thought of as strong? You're exposing your grief, your dirty laundry. Will you be still thought of as a tidy person? As a person who is capable?"

That time in my life informed my writing, and it's really informed this play. It's allowed me to take a deeper look into the loneliness of it. Some of the things in this play are absurd, and while watching some of the run-throughs, I wondered what the audience would take away from it. Would they sit there thinking, "This is not real, this is not possible, these things don't happen"? But it's all from research and from my own experience. I don't believe that a writer who decides to tackle something deeply sensitive has to tell everyone, "Hey, that's me, I went through that really terrible experience or really great experience." You don't have to tell everything about your life story. But I think for something like this that requires advocacy, it's important to share. I think, if people can, they should come forward with their own story and seek treatment. That's it. That's all I actually care about. If even one person can seek treatment from anything I'm saying or writing, honest to God, that's enough. It's such a clichéd thing, but it's true.

The point of all of it is for people who are reading and struggling to advocate for their own mental health and to seek out treatment. *Advocate for it and seek it out.* I was able to pay for treatment because of my job. Some people have to sit on waiting lists. But if you have to be on a waiting list, then you have to be on a waiting list. You can get treatment.

Since I came out to some of my close friends about my struggles, I realized how many artists are in treatment and in need of help. Many, many, many. In fact, I don't have a single close friend who hasn't sought treatment for something or other. All of us are doing it, but we're keeping it in the dark. It's very easy to say I'm getting treatment for my arthritis. It's very different to say you're getting treatment for your mental health.

It's a fascinating balance as actors, as creators, we have to keep ourselves open, keep ourselves vulnerable. It's really, really tricky because we are constantly asked to expose our most vulnerable side, our most truthful side, our most painful side. And so we have to make the choice to do it every single day. What side are you showing? I have a thousand sides that I can choose to share. Which version would you like to see?

Little Pretty and The Exceptional was first produced by Factory Theatre, Toronto, from April 1–30, 2017, with the following cast and creative team:

Dilpreet: Sugith Varughese
Simran: Farah Merani
Jasmeet: Shruti Kothari
Iyar: Shelly Antony

Director: Brendan Healy
Assistant Director: Ryan G. Hinds
Dramaturge: Iris Turcott
Production Dramaturg: Matt McGeachy
Set and Costume Designer: Yannik Larivée
Lighting Designer: André du Toit
Sound Designer: Richard Feren
Stage Manager: Laura Baxter
Apprentice Stage Manager: Michaela Steven
Head of Props and Scenic Artist: Samantha Brown
Head of Wardrobe: Chantelle Laliberte

CHARACTERS

Dilpreet: in his fifties
Simran: in her early twenties
Jasmeet: eighteen
Iyar: eighteen

TIME

Present day

SETTING

Gerrard Street, Toronto

SCENE 1

We are inside a sari shop on Gerrard Street, Toronto. There are opened and unopened boxes, saris, and mannequins everywhere. It is obvious that the store is preparing for a grand opening.

White mannequins of different sizes are displayed around the store. All are dressed in South Asian clothing. An "Opening Soon" sign can be seen in the window.

There is a picture of Guru Nanak with a garland around his neck prominently hung on the wall. There is an exit in the background that leads to the floor upstairs and the bedrooms.

DILPREET enters from the back room; he has a pile of white saris in his hands. He notices a broken male mannequin on the floor. The mannequin has face makeup on it. He drops the saris, runs to the mannequin, and screams.

DILPREET: JASMEET! Oie,[1] JASMEET! Ki karde.[2] Why you keep the door unlock? Hai?[3] Now look. That fat boy come again and all my makneek[4] is total damage.

He picks up the male mannequin.

---

1 Hey.

2 What are you doing?

3 A vocal sound. In this context it would mean "why"?

4 He means the mannequins.

I am seeing that fat boy, one tight slap I am make his white cheek red. JASMEET. Come help, na.

JASMEET enters.

Oie! Look what fat boy did. Why you keep the door open?

JASMEET: You left it unlocked. I've been upstairs in my room all day.

DILPREET: Room all day doing nothing but lazy. How many boxes you open?

JASMEET: I was working on my prom dress. I have to leave soon. What do you want?

DILPREET: Help. What you think I want? Look at what that fat boy do. Ah. Look. Boy makneek now look like girl makneek.

JASMEET: Mannequin, Dad. Not makneek.

DILPREET: Don't give me lecture. Already white makneek with Indian suit and now with red cheek. I am telling you, you better go tell that Molly lady if her son come in again and make boy to girl again, I am beat him with—

JASMEET: Just throw it out. I'll get another one from storage—

DILPREET: What *just throw*? Nothing throw. Fat loan on my head and you thinking that my money is dripping from maple tree? I am nothing throwing anything. You sit here and clean.

JASMEET: What? Dad—

DILPREET: Go get cloth and clean the girl face and make it back to boy face. I am get you Fevicol, you glue the arm together.

JASMEET: It will look ridic—

DILPREET: Store opening in five weeks and here is madam doing lazy lazy. How we open in time with so much left to do. GO—

JASMEET goes off stage to get a cloth and some glue.

JASMEET: *(off stage)* Then hire some helpers. We need it! I told you—

DILPREET: Helpers! Yes. Right. I am go to bank and say give me more money because Jassie think I am need helpers. Two daughters I am having and I am strong as bull . . . what I am need helper for?

JASMEET re-enters with a cloth and starts to clean the mannequin's face.

JASMEET: It's Magic Marker, Dad, I don't think it's coming off.

DILPREET: Try harder. When Canada flags come?

JASMEET: I just ordered them! They're not gonna deliver a hundred flags in twenty-four hours. You need to calm down. I swear it'll all get done. And you better not go to the wholesale place without me! I don't want any gold gaudy crap for the store—

DILPREET: With the rate you are disorganize I am be lucky if I am able to do store opening next year Canada Day, forget this year.

JASMEET: *(screams)* SIMMI!

DILPREET: Oie, leave her alone. She need to focus—

JASMEET: She is focused enough! She doesn't need to study for fourth year *now*!

DILPREET: She need good marks. She be big top human lawyer one day. First big top human lawyer in the full of family.

JASMEET: First: again, human-rights lawyer. Second: I don't care. SIMRAN. GET YOUR ASS DOWN HERE AND HELP DAD. I NEED TO LEAVE!

DILPREET: Watch language.

DILPREET notices how hard JASMEET is scrubbing.

And what you are scrubbing like you never drink milk. Scrub stronger.

JASMEET: Magic. Marker.

DILPREET: Put some spit on it. Spit make it faster.

DILPREET spits on the mannequin's cheek.

JASMEET: That is disgusting!

DILPREET moves about, arranging saris, mannequins, etc., around the store. SIMRAN enters. She does a tiny nervous action with her fingers—as if little ants are crawling on them. No one sees this but the audience.

SIMRAN dims the light just a little.

SIMRAN: Why is it so bright in here?

DILPREET: How it coming?

SIMRAN: Good.

SIMRAN looks at JASMEET.

DILPREET: Did you hear?

SIMRAN: No.

DILPREET: Still no?

SIMRAN: I told you, they'll email results by the end of the week. At the latest mid-next week—

JASMEET: It's not coming out, Dad!

SIMRAN: *(to JASMEET)* Nail-polish remover.

JASMEET exits to get some nail-polish remover.

DILPREET: Maybe you should call them?

SIMRAN: They're not gonna give me LSAT scores over the phone, Dad.

DILPREET: Okay. Okay. Head?

SIMRAN: Just dull . . . headache.

DILPREET: You not sleeping last night. I am hear you from my room.

SIMRAN shakes her head. Her fingers are nervous.

SIMRAN: It's . . . it's fine.

DILPREET doesn't notices as she touches her throat. It appears as if she feels like she is being choked.

I am just . . . I just . . . I'll be fine when the results are out.

DILPREET: Why you still have headache? You have too much LSIT tension. You call Doctor Saleem again right now—

SIMRAN: Dad, I am fine—

DILPREET: What fine shine—

SIMRAN: *(suddenly shouts)* I AM FINE! Stop it.

DILPREET: Aare? Why you shout now. You call him again and tell him.

SIMRAN: *(calmly)* Dad . . . I'm just . . . anxious.

DILPREET: We go see him tomorrow.

SIMRAN: I have a shift at the library—

DILPREET: We go in afternoon then.

SIMRAN: *(loving, explaining)* I need a nap, Dad. It's a no-nap headache.

JASMEET enters. She has her purse in hand and is wearing a different outfit. She hands SIMRAN the nail-polish remover.

DILPREET: *(to JASMEET)* Oie?[1]

JASMEET: *(to SIMRAN)* Happy cleaning.

DILPREET: Oie. Where you are going?

JASMEET: I told you I had to leave. Prom-committee meeting. Just for a few hours—

---

1 What are you doing?

DILPREET: No few hours. No hours. You stay here and clean.

JASMEET: Dad. I'll be right back—

She goes through a pile of brand-new Indian scarves that are packaged for sale. She looks for one to match her outfit.

DILPREET: What you are doing? Don't take brand new. And I know exactly who you are seeing. Ha? I don't like that Tamil boy. He is too Black for you.

SIMRAN: Dad!

DILPREET: All I see is his teeth.

JASMEET holds up a red scarf and a black-and-white striped scarf.

JASMEET: *(to SIMRAN)* The stripes look cooler, right?

DILPREET: You look like a zebra!

JASMEET: *(to SIMRAN)* Which one?

SIMRAN: Either.

JASMEET: Just help me pick a colour. The red matches my lips better, ya?

(to DILPREET) I won't crush it. I promise.

JASMEET takes the red one.

DILPREET: Jasmeet, you come late tonight then you have no say on sign board name. NO say. We make decision and it be final.

JASMEET: I am not gonna be late. / I promise.

JASMEET pulls out DILPREET's hidden container filled with change.

DILPREET: How many time I am hearing—

He sees her take his change.

Again, you take from my change box! Nothing you contribute, always take take take—

JASMEET: I am late. I need taxi money—

DILPREET: Why riding taxi when you have strong Punjabi legs to run. Even the cripple run in India.

JASMEET: Good for them.

JASMEET kisses DILPREET goodbye.

DILPREET: I am starting family meeting seven sharp.

JASMEET: All right. All right. I know!

DILPREET: What right? Sign-shop man complain that deadline too small for him and kept say that if Patel's son find out he now working for me, he never get hired by him.

JASMEET exits.

You better be back, Jassie!

(to SIMRAN) Why she is romancing with Tamil boy?

SIMRAN moves to the box of scarves and begins to fold and order the scarves from the darkest to the lightest colours.

I am take one look to him from the window. IN DAYLIGHT. And I am needing torch to see him. He so Black.

SIMRAN: He's so nice.

DILPREET: How you know?

SIMRAN: He's really nice to her. Jassie said so.

DILPREET: *Jassie said so!* Jasmeet brain is the size of a sugar cube. Half-melted sugar cube. You not even meet him. I see him with my own eye. He Black and teeth too white. I am find good Punjabi boy with yellow teeth like my father find your mumma.

SIMRAN smiles.

What?

SIMRAN: *(tenderly)* Mumma would be proud of you, Dad. The store is really coming along.

DILPREET: You think so?

SIMRAN nods yes.

SIMRAN: Mumma would've been really proud.

DILPREET: Good. That's good.

DILPREET notices her fidgeting with her fingers.

Why you do that with finger?

SIMRAN: What?

DILPREET: That.

He mimics SIMRAN*'s nervous fingers.*

SIMRAN: Stop doing that!

DILPREET: *(confused)* I am just showing what you keep doing. Why you upset?

Pause.

What I am say?

SIMRAN: I'm gonna go . . . I'm gonna go . . . read. I mean read. Finish studying.

DILPREET: Okay. You go studying. You go.

SIMRAN: Sorry . . .

DILPREET: You just taking too much tension your head. I am finishing here. You go upstairs and take a power nap. A powerful nap be helping.

SIMRAN exits. DILPREET watches her leave.

SCENE 2

DILPREET is pacing while holding onto a watch. SIMRAN enters.

DILPREET: *(excitedly)* Okay. All right. Here you come on time to family meeting. Jasmeet always late. But that is good now. I am have surprise for you. You excite?

SIMRAN: What is it?

DILPREET: It's surprise, Buubbla! How I am tell what it is, then it not surprise, no?

SIMRAN smiles.

SIMRAN: Okay.

DILPREET: You sit. Close eye. Okay. You excite? You ready?

She nods yes.

Here go! Bring palm. No cheat.

He places the watch in her palm.

Open.

SIMRAN opens her eyes. Beat. SIMRAN is completely taken back. DILPREET is proud of himself. He applauds.

All afternoon I am travel all the way to Brampton to get it polish. Fifty dollar it cost me.

Pause.

Look how it shine. Ha?

Beat. He can sense her hesitation.

Buubbla. *I* am give you, na. You wear it.

She gives it back.

SIMRAN: I can't. It's . . . Dad—

DILPREET: It look like it meant for your hand. I am save it for a long, long time. I am think I am give you when LSIT accepting you, but I am too excite. I am think now is better time. When you be top human lawyer you need watch. How you know time to go to court, time to go to home. How you know without watch?

SIMRAN: I have to get in first.

DILPREET: What get in? You wait till your LSIT score come. I am giving you personal guarantee you getting in and be top top human lawyer in whole of Canada soon. Our family's first. I am telling. You keep.

He puts the watch on SIMRAN.

Her fingers are nervous. She feels like she is choking, a subtle movement no one but the audience notices.

SIMRAN: It's so so beautiful.

DILPREET: It be the first thing I am buying for your mumma in Canada, no?

JASMEET enters.

See, see, see! / Always late!

JASMEET: Sorry. Sorry. Sorry. / Sorry.

DILPREET: Where is your torch?

JASMEET: What?

DILPREET: Torch. You went to see Black Tamil boy, how you see his face without torch?

DILPREET laughs and applauds at his own joke.

JASMEET: You're so racist.

DILPREET: Oie, he be *my* race. How I be racist to my race?

JASMEET: Of course you are—

DILPREET: Okay, enough with talking talking. We wait for you twenty whole minute and now you jabbering. Turn phone off. So, I am officially starting meeting.

He rings the family meeting bell.

Who doing minutes?

JASMEET: Simmi did the last one.

JASMEET gets their family meeting minutes book and takes notes during their discussion.

DILPREET: We have two topic to discuss. First: sign board name. Second: non-Black Punjabi boy for Jasmeet—

JASMEET: What?!

DILPREET: Why you are interrupt? No talking, na.

JASMEET: You are completely delirious.

DILPREET: Oie! This is my house. I am paying mortgage. So, no one using big words but me!

JASMEET: Please keep going so we're not here all night.

DILPREET: You are very excite, Jasmeet, ha?! A little bit of family interest be good, no?

JASMEET: I am *family interest*, Dad! I am here, excite and ready to vote.

DILPREET: Topic one: sign-shop man say that if I am give him the name tomorrow, he will make the sign board and do right away. That way we have board up for extra weeks *before* we open. We are needing needing to tell him tomorrow first thing morning, only because I am not having grand store Canada Day opening day with no name. Last thing I am needing is Patel's son to standing in front of my store relishing in my fail—

JASMEET's phone blasts.

Oie! You tell that Tamil teeth not to disturb.

JASMEET: It is off!

DILPREET: Here we go. I am read the list and then we vote and we are making final decision. Okay? Okay. You both better be excite. Number one: Dilpreet, Simran, and Jasmeet Company.

JASMEET: What?

DILPREET: Dilpreet, Simran and Jasmeet Company.

JASMEET: We heard you the first time. We are trying to choose a name for the sign board for a *sari store*, not a law firm.

DILPREET: Oie! Not interrupting! Number one. Dilpreet, Simran, and—

JASMEET: Stop repeating. It's horrible.

SIMRAN: The more you interrupt him the longer it will take—

DILPREET: OR OR OR OR, even better—Dilpreet, Simran, and Jasmeet AND Family Company. You like?

JASMEET & SIMRAN: NO.

DILPREET: Why?

JASMEET & SIMRAN: Next.

DILPREET: Why?

JASMEET: LAW FIRM.

SIMRAN: Next.

DILPREET: Number two. Dilpreet and Sons.

SIMRAN: What?

JASMEET: From when the hell do you have a son?

DILPREET: I know, I know, but it sounds formal, no? What you always say—cool?

JASMEET & SIMRAN: Next!

DILPREET: Why? What is wrong with that?

JASMEET: You don't have sons. THAT's what is wrong with that! Next.

DILPREET: I am not hearing you make any contribution.

JASMEET: I'm waiting my turn. Believe me, I have a phenomenal name contribution.

DILPREET: The third is my most favourite and top pick. It is a total Dilpreet Singh original. Number three:

A slight pause as he takes in the glory of this name.

Ladies Heart Happy.

He starts applauding.

JASMEET: *(simultaneously)* That's not even English. Stop clapping.

SIMRAN: *(simultaneously)* What?

DILPREET: Of course it English. Ladies Heart Happy. Those all English words.

JASMEET: It's a dumb name. What does it mean?

DILPREET: I am think, what is best creative way to make you both and my name on the sign board. So, I am think, aare,[1] make it to English—

JASMEET: You're not making any sense—

DILPREET: Ladies meaning you two. And my name . . . Dil is equal to heart in English, Preet is equal to happy in English. So—

JASMEET: *(big reaction)* AH! LADIES AND HEART HAPPY! DIL. PREET. OH, OF COURSE! THAT IS THE BEST NAME EVER! Dad, are you crazy? That sounds ridiculous! What is wrong with you? You have the worst names.

DILPREET: What you are saying? You know how long it take me to be creative and think of that name? I am think and think and think,

1 Why not?

in Punjabi maybe, but I am still think. And then, suddenly, I am thinking aare, best name for this.

SIMRAN: But it doesn't really *mean* anything—

DILPREET: What do mean it doesn't mean anything? I just explain to you—

JASMEET: No. Dad. Please.

DILPREET: It is *creative*—

JASMEET: No, it is not. It's ridiculous—

DILPREET: You both are useless. And what is your contribution? Let us hearing.

JASMEET: Get ready for your mind to be blown.

JASMEET gives the minutes book to SIMRAN.

Simmi, make sure you write this down, I've put three weeks' worth of thought into the name. So, you know how most of the stores on this strip are—

DILPREET: Just get to the name—

JASMEET: *(simultaneously)* Dad!

SIMRAN: *(simultaneously)* Dad, let her finish.

DILPREET: Hurry up.

JASMEET: So, most of the stores are typical Indian sari stores with gross, gaudy overdone shit, too much jewellery and no class. That is not our store. No. Our store is for the modern Indian woman. We are for the modern woman who does it all. We are the East meets West store. We are FUSION. Fusion, Dad. Fusion. East fusing with the West. The fusing of two world—

DILPREET: It took you three weeks to come up with this dog's urine?

JASMEET: Excuse me, I'm the one who's gonna be a fashion designer. Believe you me, the *fusion concept* is really in.

DILPREET: You only have half a brain.

SIMRAN: Ranmeet Fashion. Ran of Simran and Meet of Jasmeet. Ranmeet.

JASMEET: WHAT! Ranmeet. I love it! Listen to it—Ranmeet. That's like *real* fusion.

DILPREET: But where is me? I am missing from the name.

JASMEET: Dad, you *are* the reason we are here. So although you'll *literally* not be on that sign board, you will be. Metaphorically. You know what I mean?

DILPREET: That is worst logic. Don't try to confuse me with big word.

JASMEET: It's perfect logic and a fantastic name. Dad, please.

DILPREET: But I like Ladies Heart Happy. It include whole family.

JASMEET: Ranmeet does as well. It's the best. Dad, please—

DILPREET: But it sounds like I have a third daughter—

JASMEET: No it doesn't.

A slight pause.

Wait wait wait. What about . . . what about Ranmeet Fusions—

DILPREET: And you think my English is bad? There is no meaning in that name—

SIMRAN: It's a good name. It works.

DILPREET: But with Ladies Heart Happy I can have a good logo. L.H.H. Logo is very important, ha.

JASMEET: R.F. will look really cool, Dad. I'll make a design that will look like—

JASMEET notices SIMRAN wearing the watch.

Where did you get that?

Beat.

Why are you wearing her watch?

Beat. SIMRAN's fingers are nervous.

DILPREET: How it matter, Jassie—

JASMEET: Where did you get that?

SIMRAN: Dad gave it to me.

JASMEET: What? Why?

Beat.

(to DILPREET) Why did you give it to her?

SIMRAN: Jassie—

JASMEET: *(to SIMRAN)* Shut up, Simran.

(to DILPREET) Why did you give it to her?

Pause.

Dad?

DILPREET: Jassie.

SIMRAN: Just leave it, Jassie—

JASMEET: I am not speaking to you, Simran! Where did it even come from?

DILPREET: I was cleaning. I found it. So I give it. End discussion. So, what is the final decision on the name then?

JASMEET: *You found it so you give it?* Dad, why is it even in our house? You told me that you threw that crazy woman's shit out years ago—

DILPREET: Watch your mouth, Jasmeet. You not call your mumma that—

JASMEET: *(sharply)* Why have you kept it?

DILPREET tries to make it casual.

DILPREET: It's okay, na, Jassie. It's the only thing I have left from her, the only thing I keep, no? It look good on Simran.

JASMEET: *(to DILPREET)* No it doesn't.

(to SIMRAN) Take it off.

Pause.

Take it off.

SIMRAN: Jassie, please—

JASMEET: Take it off, Simran, please.

Beat.

Take it off.

SIMRAN: I don't want to.

Beat.

JASMEET storms out.

Beat.

Yelling, DILPREET exits behind her.

DILPREET: Jasmeet, you come back here. She is older to you. Have respect.

Beat. SIMRAN is alone. SIMRAN looks at the watch and touches the dial for a beat. She brings the dial up to her ear to listen to the ticking watch.

SCENE 3

Two a.m. Night sounds can be heard. The store lights are completely dark. A slight moment of stillness. A small light is turned on. SIMRAN *walks in with a university course catalogue. She looks confused and out of place. She looks around to check her surroundings. She is looking at the saris and the boxes everywhere. She touches them. She has never seen them before. She looks at the watch. She touches her throat. She stands still. Beat. Back in reality she knows where she is. She starts to look through the book and highlight specific courses. She softly sings a lullaby to herself.*

SIMRAN: Lalla lalla loori, doodh ki katori, doodh may batasha, Simran kare tamasha.

Beat.

Lalla lalla loori, doodh ki katori, doodh may batasha, Simran kare tamasha.

She stops and looks up. She is quiet as she listens. She listens really carefully. She looks at her watch. She looks around. All she sees around her are open cardboard boxes filled with expensive saris. She starts to read again.

SCENE 4

JASMEET *is searching for the change box.* DILPREET *enters holding a box of clothing for the store.*

JASMEET: LOOK LOOK LOOK what I have for you!!! But, first, I need money for supplies.

DILPREET: I keep it in secret for a reason, Jassie.

JASMEET: Dad, trust me, you want to give me money right now. You will die when you see what I am holding! I had a really good marketing idea for our store.

DILPREET: What market?

JASMEET: Not market. Marketing. Iyar and I worked on it for hours—

DILPREET: Again you talk to Tamil—

JASMEET: Uff, Dad. So Iyar came up with a brilliant idea. Well, originally I came up with it but he added some amazing details. He's a genius. So, he's the prom committee's main graphic designer and—

DILPREET: What prawn?

JASMEET: PROM. It's a big event thing . . . dance thing . . . I told you, remember? . . . For school. Anyway, so, because he is such a good graphic designer, he said he would create flyers for Ranmeet Fusions and we could colour photocopy hundreds of them and distribute them all around the neighbourhood.

Pause. DILPREET *pays attention.*

Yes. You see how fantastic that idea is! So, Iyar was on Skype with me all morning working on this flyer AND here is the final version.

She pulls out the flyer. DILPREET *is impressed.*

Look, look how the logo looks. Just look at it! It's a Jasmeet Singh original, thank you very much!

DILPREET *notices a map.*

DILPREET: I am liking map.

JASMEET: That was Iyar's idea too. He insisted that we create a mini map, just to make sure that people know *exactly* where we're located.

DILPREET: Tamil have good brain behind that white teeth.

JASMEET: Of course he does, Dad. He is this year's valedictorian and I am sure he'll be the prom king. He is seriously smart, Dad. This font is something he created, by the way. He has this software—

Terrified, SIMRAN *enters. She is holding a letter.*

Simmi, look what— what's wrong?

SIMRAN: Eighty-two.

JASMEET: What?

SIMRAN: Eighty-two.

DILPREET: Eighty-two what?

SIMRAN: Eighty-two.

DILPREET: What you are saying?

SIMRAN: *(to herself)* How did this happen?

DILPREET: LSIT! Simmi! This is good news. / This is such good—

JASMEET: *(internal)* Shit shit shit shit!

SIMRAN: Osgoode is not gonna happen. Osgoode is not gonna happen.

JASMEET: It's fine—

SIMRAN: *(to herself)* How did I get this number?

DILPREET: What fine? It's great. That is fantas. That is a good number. We should having some celebrate—

JASMEET: It's fine.

SIMRAN: Fine? It's not the top-ten percentile. It's not. I wanna go to Osgoode, the best school. The best school. I can't get in with this number. They don't accept eighty-two—

JASMEET: You said you can take it again?

DILPREET: What? It's good mark. Why you need again?

SIMRAN: ARE YOU NOT LISTENING TO ME! It's not!

JASMEET: No, it's not, Dad.

DILPREET: Why not? It high score—

JASMEET: Dad, it's just . . . not. They need above ninety-five—

DILPREET: But that high score . . . no?

JASMEET shakes her head no.

But how you get such low mark then? You study so much—

SIMRAN bursts out in anger.

SIMRAN: I know that! Don't you think I know that? I know that! Shit. Shit. Shit.

JASMEET: Simmi, you'll be fine!

SIMRAN: What's going to happen?

DILPREET: Simmi, listen to me—

SIMRAN: No. Dad. I have to get it. I have to do it. I have to get in.

JASMEET: You'll get in—

SIMRAN: I have to!

JASMEET: You will, Simmie!

SIMRAN: *(internal)* Shit—

JASMEET: Lots of people take it more than once. You'll do it again. Just take those LSAT prep classes.

Beat.

SIMRAN: Yes yes yes yes, you're right! I will. And and . . . I'm . . . I *am* going to . . . I am going to take those LSAT test prep classes. They have them. I am gonna to do all thosc classes and learn the strategies on how to get above ninety-five and I'm gonna get in. I'll do it. I'll get brilliant marks. I can do it. I need to check . . . check when I can sign up. I'm gonna do it.

JASMEET: Exactly. So, it's fine.

SIMRAN sits. Her mind is racing.

Okay, so, in happy news, look at this flyer!

JASMEET shows the map to SIMRAN.

Concept and design by me and Iyar did the actual font and format stuff. What do you think?

SIMRAN looks at JASMEET.

Check out the map. It's 3D. What do you think?

SIMRAN doesn't look at it. She stares out for a beat. She exits.

Okay, I'm gonna get these photocopied and—

She sees the expression of DILPREET's face.

It happens all the time, Dad. She'll take it again. She'll get in. She's exceptional. Now, give me some money for the photocopy.

I won't be late.

DILPREET gives JASMEET money. She kisses him goodbye.

DILPREET nods. JASMEET exits.

SCENE 5

SIMRAN's laptop sits on a counter. JASMEET is laughing. IYAR is wearing a very expensive traditional Indian wedding turban on his head and pretending to be on a horse.

They're seriously flirting.

IYAR: I LOOK HOT!

JASMEET continues laughing.

JASMEET: You look gross!

IYAR: Gross?

JASMEET: There is no way I am going with you like that.

IYAR: I look *hot*, thank you. I should rent a horse. We can make an entrance. Now THAT, that'll be a prom to remember.

JASMEET: If you wear it, I'll go with Saacha Singh.

IYAR: Oh please. Moustache Singh can't even dance and looks like a douche.

JASMEET: Not only is he handsome AND smart, he also *owns* a car.

IYAR: That's his brother, cross-eyed-weirdo Singh's car—

JASMEET: Same thing!

IYAR: Wait, you think he's hot?

JASMEET: Are you jealous?

IYAR: Ya right.

JASMEET: I think you are.

IYAR: Moustache Singh ain't got nothin' on me. I got them abs, baby! Have you told your dad yet?

JASMEET: Not yet.

IYAR: So how are we gonna go?

> *IYAR smiles. He pulls her in by her belt buckle. Their noses touch. They kiss. He kisses her again. They enjoy it. They pull apart. She touches his face.*

JASMEET: Of course we're gonna go! That prom queen crown was made for my head.

IYAR: So then?

JASMEET: Don't worry, you just wait and watch.

Hi, dad!

DILPREET enters. He is holding a bag filled with small Canadian flags. IYAR awkwardly takes the expensive marriage turban off.

DILPREET: Get me Crush cola. It is blistering outside.

JASMEET exits. Pause. DILPREET puts his stuff down and walks up to IYAR, takes the expensive marriage turban from his hands, and puts it back in the protective covering.

IYAR: Sorry. I was just . . . we were just. I am . . . my name is Iyar. I am just . . .

DILPREET stares at him. An extended pause.

DILPREET: What is your father's name?

IYAR: Sorry?

DILPREET stares.

Oh. Um . . . Ramakrishna Balasubramaniam Iyar.

DILPREET: Tamil Nadu or Kerala.

IYAR: . . . Tamil Nadu.

DILPREET: Passport.

IYAR: Sorry?

DILPREET stares.

Sorry, what?!

DILPREET stares.

Oh . . . passport, yes. I'm from here. I live here . . . I mean, I was born here.

DILPREET stares, fascinated.

DILPREET: What your teeth guy's name?

IYAR: What . . . what do you mean?

DILPREET: Dentist. What your dentist name? Why your teeth so white?

JASMEET re-enters.

JASMEET: Iyar, this is my dad, the greatest father ever. And THIS is Iyar. I was telling you about him, Dad, remember? He even made that map you loved. He is one of our top athletes AND he's been accepted to U of T for biochemistry. He gets better grades than me!

DILPREET: Any lightbulb get better grade than you.

JASMEET: So you wanna know what we *toiled* over all afternoon for the store? You ready for this? Tell him.

IYAR: It's okay, you can tell him.

JASMEET gives IYAR a shut-up-and-do-as-I-say look.

DILPREET starts to leave.

DILPREET: When you are done your chit chat, call me.

JASMEET: No, Dad, stop it. Listen.

IYAR: So, umm . . . My uncle has a restaurant. An Indian, like South Indian, restaurant—right downtown. It's not as famous yet as Bombay Palace but I am sure you've heard of it. It's called Castle Nadu. Like: Tamil Nadu?

DILPREET: Never heard of it.

IYAR: Right. Okay. So, one thing that my brother and I help him with is . . . is a software we developed for his inventory. What I mean by that is—

DILPREET: I am not born inside a sewage drain. I am know inventory meaning. Keep proceed.

IYAR: Sorry. Right. So my brother and I help him maintain a really tight inventory of what's coming into the restaurant and what's being sold, damaged, etc. It is a really useful system that we developed. So, when J mentioned—Jasmeet mentioned—your store not having an inventory system, I thought, why not share that software with you. You know?

JASMEET: Anyway, the point is this afternoon Iyar spent all his time downloading and updating this software onto Simran's new laptop—

DILPREET: She told you not to touch it. Where she be?

JASMEET: Library shift. So, as I was saying, Iyar has GREAT software for our inventory—

DILPREET: I am have a book and pencil—

JASMEET: You need to move with the times. Seriously. You said that you will not hire help, at least for the first year. Iyar is volunteering his time to help you, Dad!

DILPREET looks at IYAR. Pause. He continues to look.

IYAR: Right. Okay. Well, it was nice to meet you, Uncle. It's . . . it's ready to use. Let me know what you think of the software. Thanks. Thank you. Bye.

IYAR exits.

JASMEET: He is a really nice guy, Dad. And you know, he might be *lucky enough* to go to the prom with me. I mean a lot of guys are *begging* to go with me, but, you know, biochemistry at U of T. That's like legit smart. It makes no sense if I don't pick him. Right?

DILPREET: Flags are here, sort them to hang.

She finds the bag of flags and opens them. She's elated.

(exiting) Why his teeth so bright? Find out. Find out who the dentist is.

JASMEET: Uff, Dad. Please.

JASMEET takes out a couple of flags, looks at them, and makes a garland pattern. Suddenly she notices something on SIMRAN's computer screen. Beat.

She looks carefully. She looks surprised and confused. Beat.

SCENE 6

Later that night. There are a few Canadian flag streamers hanging around the store. SIMRAN *is sitting cross-legged on the store counter. She is reading. She stops and looks at one of the streamers moving in the wind. From her point of view she sees her dead mother hanging. The image disappears. She is suddenly in a different zone. She feels out of her body. She listens to her watch. Pause. She looks at the same spot. It's just a Canadian flag streamer, not her dead mother. She gets up and tugs on the flags. She touches her neck. She feels displaced.*

She's cold.

SCENE 7

The next afternoon SIMRAN *sits waiting for* JASMEET*. "Pretty Woman" from the Indian movie* Kal Ho Naa Ho *plays.*

JASMEET: *(off stage)* Almost almost . . .

A moment passes.

SIMRAN: JASSIE!

JASMEET: *(off stage)* WAIT! Two seconds.

A moment passes.

(off stage) Are you ready? Hit it.

SIMRAN: It's already playing.

JASMEET: *(off stage)* I know, but make it louder!

SIMRAN turns the music up. JASMEET enters wearing a beautiful fuchsia prom dress. She holds a brooch of artificial black flowers.

What do you think? What do you think? What do you think? Short but classy. Right?

They smile at each other.

Am I brilliant or what?

SIMRAN: Brilliant.

JASMEET: Ahhh!

JASMEET starts to dance and sing to the music. She dances around SIMRAN and SIMRAN joins her. It's a beautiful sisterly moment.

(matter-of-fact) Damn, I look stunning! Iyar is one lucky guy to be taking the best-dressed girl to prom. But, okay, here is the thing, flower or no flower. I mean, I don't want to make it too much, and I want Iyar's flower in the pocket thingy to match mine, and he's not gonna wear a black flower. What do you think?

She holds up the flowers with the dress.

What? Too much?

SIMRAN: Put it near your waist.

JASMEET: That's stupid.

SIMRAN: Just do it.

She places the flowers near the waist of the dress.

That looks nice—

JASMEET looks at herself.

JASMEET: It does! Simmi, it totally does! Now, imagine me looking like this with the *prom queen* crown on my head.

SIMRAN touches her neck and slightly flinches.

Did you sleep last night?

SIMRAN nods yes. She touches her throat.

And what the fuck are you doing with your throat?

SIMRAN: What?

JASMEET: You keep touching it.

Beat.

You're having nightmares again, aren't you? I know you are.

SIMRAN: Stop it.

JASMEET: Simmi.

SIMRAN: What?

JASMEET: Are you?

SIMRAN: I don't like it when you do that—

JASMEET: Do what? And take off that watch, it's stupid.

SIMRAN: I like it.

JASMEET: No you don't.

SIMRAN: I like it. I remember it on Mumma's wrist.

JASMEET: You really wanna walk around wearing that fucking maniac's watch? And when did you put that picture of her up as your screen saver?

Beat.

Simmi?

SIMRAN: I am gonna fail the LSATs again

JASMEET: You didn't fail, Simmi, you just got a shitty grade.

SIMRAN: I can feel it, and then it will all be a waste—

JASMEET: You won't. You'll take it again and get a higher percentile. That's all. Sign up for the classes and you'll be fine.

Beat.

What?

Beat.

SIMRAN: I am scared.

JASMEET: Scared of what?

Beat.

SIMRAN: The library has the new *Cosmo*?

JASMEET takes it in.

JASMEET: The hair issue?

SIMRAN nods yes.

Can you get it?

SIMRAN: Have it on hold for you.

JASMEET: Thank you, thank you! You're the fucking best!

SIMRAN: What shoes are you gonna wear?

JASMEET: I don't know. I'll borrow something from Roop's closet.

SIMRAN: No, you need new shoes. It's prom!

JASMEET: Umm hello? Do you know how expensive this fabric was? This babe is outta juice!

SIMRAN: No. You need new shoes.

JASMEET: I'm not wasting—

SIMRAN: You're not going to prom in borrowed shoes.

SIMRAN takes money out of her purse.

Get something with sparkles.

JASMEET: SIMMI! You're my favourite sister!

SIMRAN: I know.

JASMEET: Ah! I forgot tell you. So, Iyar said . . . well, it's not just his idea, prom night we were all thinking of going to a hotel after.

Just for drinks, and Iyar was saying if all our friends pitch in a little money together then we can rent a suite.

Pause.

You wanna come to the after-party?

SIMRAN shakes her head no.

You might like it.

SIMRAN: No.

JASMEET: Just come. I told Roop you might come and her hot cousin Amar is gonna be there. I think he likes you. He keeps asking—

SIMRAN: I said NO!

JASMEET: Okay! You'll miss a great party.

Pause.

What else do I need?

SIMRAN: Nothing. It's perfect. You look prefect. It's . . . ya, perfect.

They smile.

JASMEET exits. SIMRAN sits. She holds her head for a beat. She looks up. Beat. She has to pee really badly. But she will not let herself do it. She pushes at her crotch with her hand and squeezes her thighs. Suddenly she feels like her bladder will explode.

She inhales and holds her breath. She will not pee.

SCENE 8

The next day, late evening. DILPREET *enters dragging a massive sign that reads "Ranmeet Fusions" in English and Punjabi.*

DILPREET: Look look look! Aare![1] Where is everyone? Look what I am bring! Simmi. Jassie.

JASMEET: *(off stage)* Iyar?

DILPREET: Me. Come down.

JASMEET: *(off stage, shouts)* I am doing my makeup!

He places the sign and admires it.

DILPREET: Aare, coming now, Jassie! I am bringing signboard. Simmi, I am bringing your favourite laddoo[2] with cashews to celebrate.

A pause. He looks at it some more.

Bring Crush cola, I am blistering!

Pause.

Where you two?

JASMEET: *(off stage)* Coming!

He admires the sign. A moment later JASMEET *enters with a Crush pop for* DILPREET. *She is stunned by the board.*

1 Ooh my God.

2 An Indian sweet.

WHAT. WHAT. WHAT. WHAT. WHAT. OH MY GOD! OH. MY. GOD. Dad! Oh God! Dad, that looks amazing! Look at it! Fuck. Shit. Sorry! I mean—

DILPREET: Where is Simmi?

JASMEET: Library shift. That looks phenomenal. The colours are awesome. I am sooo glad I chose green.

DILPREET: Good choosing.

JASMEET: Look at the logo! Am I the best designer or what? Shit. Dad!

Beat.

You did good. You did really really good.

DILPREET: *(with pride)* I am do good, hah?! Ha! I am do good!

JASMEET nods yes.

Look how solid that be. Like, how you always say? Bollywood meeting Hollywood style, na? Sign-shop man tell me no one, not one person on the whole of the Gerrard Street, or even in whole of the Toronto city, have a sign that this solid. He say, in the evening when we be lighting it, even look *more* solid.

He calls out.

SIMMI!

JASMEET: She has a shift, Dad.

They admire the sign. She hugs her dad. A pure moment of love.

Can I just say . . . and I know, I know, I know you hate it when I speak like this, but I have to say it: Patel's son can go fuck himself.

DILPREET: Jassie!

JASMEET: I know! I am sorry, okay. But I just have to say it. Once he sees this, he'll have no idea what hit him! Seriously! What did he think? He would kick you out after you worked YEARS for his dead dad building their goddamn store and you would, what? Beg on the streets? Not be able to open your own store? What an asshole.

DILPREET: His father was a good man.

JASMEET: A good man who couldn't raise a son.

There is a knock on the front door. IYAR enters.

IYAR: Oh, sorry—

JASMEET: Close your eyes.

IYAR: What?

JASMEET: Your eyes. Close them. Close!

IYAR closes his eyes. JASMEET grabs him by his shoulders and places him in front of the signboard.

Open.

IYAR opens his eyes. He is excited by how great the sign looks.

IYAR: Oh wow!

JASMEET: I know, right!

IYAR: It looks . . . it looks amazing.

JASMEET: It does. It does. It does.

DILPREET: When her shift end? Call her.

JASMEET: *(to DILPREET)* I will. Just a sec.

(to IYAR) Okay, look how perfectly the logo turned out. It looks hot, doesn't it?

IYAR: *(to JASMEET)* It really does.

A slight pause.

(to DILPREET) It looks amazing, Uncle.

DILPREET nods with a hint of a smile.

If I may make a suggestion . . . I think . . . along with this signboard you should have a sidewalk sign too. To attract customers from a distance.

DILPREET just looks at him.

JASMEET: What? That's a great idea!

DILPREET: I am not having a tree dripping with dollar bills in my back pocket to get another made.

IYAR: No no no, you don't have to make it; it's a simple chalkboard sign. We have an extra from the restaurant. I can bring it in.

DILPREET: You think I am running on donation?

JASMEET: *(to DILPREET)* Uff! Dad, please! It's a great idea.

(to IYAR*)* Yes, bring it in. I'll do a good drawing on it.

DILPREET: *(to* IYAR*)* Did you eat?

> *IYAR is taken aback by the question but doesn't show it to DILPREET.*

IYAR: Yes, Uncle.

DILPREET: I am bring laddoo to celebrate. They are Simmi's favourite. Open bag. Eat some. Simmi . . .

> *JASMEET opens the bag filled with laddoos and they all take one. Suddenly the door opens and SIMRAN barges in. She is panting as she clutches her purse. She bolts the door shut. For a slight moment she looks stunned. She checks the locks.*

SIMRAN: The fat kid . . . Dad, the fat kid has gone crazy.

DILPREET: *(simultaneously)* What is / happen?

JASMEET: *(simultaneously)* What the hell? / What happened?

SIMRAN: The fat kid, he was just . . . was just . . . I was crossing. I was crossing Gerrard and Rhodes and I saw him across the street. And he was . . . he was . . . I was crossing Gerrard and Rhodes and he was looking at me from across the street. He was on Gerrard and Rhodes. On Rhodes. He was just looking and so . . . so I . . . so I . . . so I was on Rhodes—

DILPREET: Okay, you sit down and tell me what fat boy did—

SIMRAN: LISTEN. LISTEN. Listen. Dim it. Dim dim it.

> *DILPREET dims the lights.*

He was on Rhodes and he was waving . . . to me . . . at me . . . and then he just turned like a like a like wild . . . like a wild dog. He was just so angry. He was on Rhodes. So I so I—

DILPREET: So then what happen?

JASMEET: What are you—

SIMRAN: I was running and he was suddenly running. Fast. Like, he was running fast, Dad. Behind me.

DILPREET: That Molly lady bastard son—

JASMEET: Simmi, he can't—

SIMRAN: So close, Dad. I could, I could feel his breath on my . . . He was first standing on Rhodes and then I could feel his breath on my neck. I turned around and he was running so fast, Dad—

JASMEET: He can't . . . he's so fat he can't even walk properly—

SIMRAN: He was. He was running! He was so angry—

JASMEET: But he can't—

SIMRAN: SHUT UP. He was he was he was he was he was . . .

JASMEET: This is Iyar.

Pause.

IYAR: Hi—

SIMRAN: *(as if she can't hear)* What?

JASMEET: Iyar. I told you. This is Iyar.

SIMRAN: *(to IYAR)* What?

JASMEET: Simmi. He is here with me.

SIMRAN: What?

SIMRAN looks at IYAR. JASMEET has had enough. SIMRAN is suddenly fully aware of her surroundings.

JASMEET: *(to IYAR)* This is my sister. Simran.

IYAR smiles.

IYAR: Sorry about the kid. You want me to go beat him up?

Pause.

JASMEET: He's funny, right?

She notices the signboard.

SIMRAN: It's green.

IYAR: I should—I'll get going. Thank you.

JASMEET unbolts the locks.

(as he exits) It looks really great, Uncle.

DILPREET nods in thanks.

JASMEET: Two seconds . . . I'll be back.

JASMEET and IYAR exit. SIMRAN bolts the door immediately behind them.

SIMRAN: I bought you laddoo. With cashews.

She hands him a box of laddoos. She exits. DILPREET *stands beside the signboard. It looks like his world is crumbling around him.* DILPREET *pick up the phone and dials a number. Mid-dial he stops and hangs up.*

DILPREET: *(shouting off stage)* Simmi, there is daal in the fridge.

SCENE 9

The next morning, around 6 a.m. SIMRAN *is in the same outfit as in the last scene. She is working on her computer with extraordinary focus. The U of T course catalogue and piles of papers are scattered all around her.* DILPREET *enters, having just woken up from sleep.*

DILPREET: Simmi, what you are doing so early?

Pause.

What you are doing, Simmi—

SIMRAN: Shhh.

DILPREET: Simmi?

Pause. He stands there watching her as she keeps working.

SIMRAN: Wait, I said.

A moment. She finishes what she is doing and double checks the paper.

I signed up. There was limited space, but I'm in. I signed up for the LSAT prep classes. I need to go.

DILPREET: Where?

SIMRAN: College Street. Right now. Drive me. Now. Let's go.

DILPREET: What?

SIMRAN: College Street bookstore. U of T Bookstore. Drive me.

DILPREET: Simmi—

SIMRAN: To get my workbooks. For the prep class.

DILPREET: It's six in the morning.

SIMRAN: I DON'T CARE. DRIVE ME, DAMN IT! I NEED TO GO. RIGHT NOW.

DILPREET: Why you are shout?

SIMRAN: *(immediately calm)* I need to go now, Dad.

DILPREET: Simmi—

SIMRAN: 214 College Street. College Street and St. George Street. Near Beverley Street. Just pass Ross Street. I just signed up for LSAT prep classes and need my workbooks. I need them, to study them, before I start, Dad. I need them. Now.

DILPREET: Yes. Okay. I am take you, Simmi, but it too early. I am take you when it open—

SIMRAN: Monday to Friday: 8:45 a.m. to 6 p.m. There will be a line. If we leave now, then we'll get there by 6:30. We can stand in line. I want to be first in line. So, let's go right now.

DILPREET: Why you are getting too much—

SIMRAN: Why are you not listening to me? Will you drive me now or no?

DILPREET: No!

She starts to leave.

Stop it right now! You're not going anywhere. What is the matter—

SIMRAN: NOTHING. NOTHING IS THE MATTER! I NEED MY WORKBOOKS!

DILPREET: We will get them! You need to—

SIMRAN: Don't do that. Don't tell me what to do.

DILPREET: You are taking too much tension. I am noticing you for the last few day. You are—

SIMRAN: What are you noticing? There is nothing to notice—

DILPREET: Simmi, I am not liking this, I am tell you. You are not sleeping again and your headache is back—

SIMRAN: Stop it. Stop it.

DILPREET: Now we call Doctor Saleem and we go in—

SIMRAN panics.

SIMRAN: If I don't get these workbooks then I am going to fail again. I'm gonna fail, Dad! I'm gonna fail! I'm gonna fail us! I'm gonna fail! I'm gonna fail!

DILPREET: You are never fail anything ever. What are you even—

SIMRAN: I need to do this. I am going. I am going. I am going . . . Dad . . . Stop. Stop. Stop. Stop. Make it stop. Please.

DILPREET: What?

SIMRAN: Stop. Stop. Stop it. Make it stop.

DILPREET: What you want me to make stop—

SIMRAN pees herself. She stands in the pool of her urine. Beat. Beat. Beat.

(strict) Go take a bath and clean yourself up. Then get some sleep. No discussion. Go now.

(gently) Get some sleep.

Beat. SIMRAN exits. Beat. DILPREET gets a cloth and wipes up the mess.

SCENE 10

Same day. 8:24 a.m. SIMRAN enters an otherwise empty stage. She looks at her watch.

SIMRAN: 8:24 . . . 8:24 . . . 8:24 . . .

She repeats this over and over again.

Her hair is soaking wet. She is wearing a winter jacket. She goes to DILPREET's hidden money box and takes out a couple of bills. Beat. She places the box distractedly on the table. She exits.

SCENE 11

That night. Midnight. DILPREET *is pacing while he speaks on the phone.* JASMEET *sits.*

DILPREET: Don't you keep telling me you *let me know soon*! When *soon*?! I am sit here and I am wait for the last four hours and not one police persons is calling me back!

Listens.

What you all are doing there?

Listens.

I am do bullshit with "it take time." Work faster! You find my daughter immediately and you call me back!

Listens.

NO! Don't raising voice. I am not deaf!

JASMEET: Dad! Don't harass—

DILPREET: I am needing you to find her. I am going to keep calling every fifteen minute. I am told you seven hundred times SHE IS HAVING LONG HAIR. LONG BLACK HAIR.

Listens.

BLACK BLACK BLACK! Learn some English!

JASMEET: Stop it!

JASMEET *yanks the phone from her father's hand.*

Hi, I am so sorry! My dad's . . .

Sorry!

DILPREET: *(simultaneously)* Tell her my taxes is paying her salary!

JASMEET: *(simultaneously)* Sorry again!

Listens.

Ya, I know. But it's not like her to just disappear.

Listens.

So, we're very—

Listens.

Yes, well . . . we already told the officer.

Listens.

Ya, my dad was the last person to see her . . .

Listens.

Here in the house. Ya.

Listens.

He told me they had a fight. / She—

DILPREET: It has nothing to do with fight!

JASMEET listens.

JASMEET: Maybe . . . But she doesn't have many friends.

Listens.

Okay . . . Thank you. Yes. No, we'll stay off the phone.

Listens.

Thanks.

She hangs up. A slight pause.

DILPREET: You call Tamil and ask him to come over. He and I go on foot to find her.

JASMEET: Dad, it's midnight! I'm not calling him. You're not going walking all over Gerrard—

DILPREET: Do it! He is good boy, he help—

JASMEET: I'm not . . . stop it.

DILPREET paces.

DILPREET: Try her cell again. Leave message again!

JASMEET: Her voicemail is full.

From her cellphone JASMEET calls SIMRAN again. Voicemail. She hangs up.

Extended pause. DILPREET keeps pacing.

DILPREET: I am have better plan now. Call Tamil, tell him come stay here so you not alone. I go walking to find her. That be better plan. These white people police never help us. I know.

JASMEET: Dad, listen to me. You're not gonna go looking for her in the dark, and if the cops come you have to be here.

DILPREET: Call the bookstore again.

JASMEET: Dad, when you were there they told you a hundred times, there is no way for them to keep track of customers coming in and out. They have no idea if she was there.

DILPREET: They wrong. What if they wrong—

JASMEET: Dad—

DILPREET: Maybe she at the library?

JASMEET: How many more times . . . she wasn't supposed to work today. It's closed.

DILPREET: How you know?

JASMEET: It's midnight!

DILPREET: How? How she leave? Where she go? I am in the house all day. How?

He paces. Beat. Beat. Beat.

(suddenly, panicked) What if she never come back to me?

JASMEET: Dad, stop! / She'll come back. I am sure she's—

DILPREET: No. What if she . . . then am lost both. / It's my fault.

JASMEET: Dad, you're . . . / Sit down. Please. Dad. Please.

DILPREET: Jassi. Jassi. Jassi. Jassi. / Oh my God.

JASMEET: Dad, please. Breathe. Stop. / Calm down.

DILPREET: Check the news. She is dead—

JASMEET: Don't even—

DILPREET: If someone kill her . . . check it. I am say check the news check, people bury her in backyard, throw her in a trunk . . .

JASMEET notices DILPREET's money box on the table.

This is like Mumma. This like when Mumma gone . . . disappear and I am wait and wait and wait. Police bring her back. I so scared then. When Mumma—

JASMEET puts it together.

JASMEET: Dad . . . Dad . . . I . . . She took a cab.

JASMEET bolts towards the door.

I know where she went—

DILPREET: What? Where . . .

As JASMEET exits:

JASMEET: You just stay . . . stay here. You have to stay here for the police.

JASMEET exits. DILPREET calls after her:

DILPREET: Jassie, Jasmeet . . . wait. Jasmeet!

DILPREET looks lost.

SCENE 12

DILPREET is on the floor.

DILPREET: Waheguru Ji Ka Khalsa. Waheguru ji ki Fateh . . . Waheguru Ji Ka Khalsa. Waheguru ji ki Fateh . . .

He repeats the prayer over and over again. The front door opens.

JASMEET and SIMRAN enter. SIMRAN looks disoriented and is shaking. As soon as they enter DILPREET walks up to SIMRAN and slaps her hard across the face. There is a stunned silence.

Beat. Beat. Beat.

DILPREET speaks to JASMEET as he looks at SIMRAN.

Jassie, go to kitchen and make her some tea and butter toast.

JASMEET: Dad . . .

DILPREET: Go.

JASMEET: Let her—

DILPREET: Right now.

Beat.

JASMEET leaves.

Beat.

(gently) Where you be, Buubbla?

Beat.

Where you be?

Beat. Beat. Beat.

SIMRAN: 8:24.

DILPREET: What? Where you go for so long? Where you go?

Beat.

(verbal slap) Answer me, Simran.

SIMRAN: 8:24. I went to see her tonight. In our old house. Our backyard. 147 Eighth Street. Her chestnut tree. 147 Eighth Street. The hanging tree. It is still there, Dad, in the backyard of our old house. 147 Eighth Street. Red sari with yellow border with golden trim. She was swaying, Dad. Bindi in place. Her hair is parted . . . covered in . . . coconut oil.

As she says "back and forth" DILPREET *pulls out his phone and dials a number.*

I watched her swaying. Back and forth, back and forth, back and forth, back and forth, back and forth, back and forth, back and forth, back and forth, back and forth.

She exits as she continues saying "back and forth." DILPREET*'s call goes to voice mail.*

DILPREET: Doctor Saleem, this Dilpreet leaving you message. I am come with Simmi early tomorrow to you. She is not right . . . She not right in the head.

Beat. He hangs up.

SCENE 13

JASMEET and DILPREET are in the middle of a heated argument. The scene begins mid-conversation.

DILPREET: I told you to wake her up and tell her to get ready. Listen to me! Saleem say she *needs* to go now! He just calling me back to say to bringing her in now. Right now!

JASMEET: No, Dad—

DILPREET: She needs this, Jassie—

JASMEET: No she doesn't! This'll make it worse—

DILPREET: She is going wrong in the head—

JASMEET: Dad, nothing is wrong with her! She's just stressed, and you know why she is getting even more stressed? Because of you! Lawyer lawyer lawyer, that's what you keep saying to / her.

DILPREET: I am say? I am say / nothing—

JASMEET: Yes you do. You say that all / the time—

DILPREET: It is SHE who wanting to be lawyer—

JASMEET: Exactly, and she needs to do the extra courses, take the exam, get into law school, and she'll be fine again.

DILPREET: Fine? Jassie, she is not right in the head. How many times I am tell you. She is not right—

JASMEET: It's stress, Dad—

DILPREET: You remember how Mumma became crazy—

JASMEET: What the fuck do I remember, Dad? I was six when she killed herself. I remember fuck all! But I *know* she was crazy. But that's not Simmi!

DILPREET: That's *not* Simmi? You know what she do yesterday . . . where she went, yes?

JASMEET: Yes, I'm the one who figured it out, who brought her back, remember?

DILPREET: Why . . . why if she not going crazy, why say that she *seeing* her. She is *seeing* Mumma hanging. With her own two eyes . . .

JASMEET: Of course she said she is seeing Mumma. She went to the fucking house so she is remembering Mumma hanging. And thanks to that stupid fucking watch of yours that's all that's on her mind. She put pictures of Mumma as her laptop screen saver . . . I saw it.

DILPREET: Jassie, listen to me. I am hear with my own two ears last night, she say that she *saw* Mumma is swaying back and forth . . . over and over. She say she *saw* Mumma in sari, her hair, her oil. Every . . . every thing. Something big wrong, Jassie—

JASMEET: *(justifying)* Dad, do you know *how many* people experience auditory hallucinations when they're anxious? I looked it up last night. It happens, Dad. During anxiety . . . during panic—

DILPREET: When Mumma going mental—

JASMEET: SHE IS NOT LIKE MUMMA! STOP COMPARING—

DILPREET: When Mumma going mental I am not being able to help. I am keep working day and night in Patel's store for money and I am not even know what happen. She keep talking to people that not even real or don't talk at all. I am not taking Mumma to a doctor. Or to a hospital. I am not to make that mistake again. I am not—

JASMEET: They will put her in isolation and lock her away. Is that what you fucking want—

DILPREET: I am not going to stand here and argue with your half brain. Simran needing to go and get help. I am not wanting *another* death on my head.

JASMEET: And that is *exactly* what you're going to get. And it will be *your* fault.

Beat.

Do you want that?

Beat.

DILPREET: Jasmeet.

JASMEET: She *will*, Dad. Your biggest fear *will* come true. Listen to me. She *will* kill herself, just like Mumma. Do you want that?

Beat.

Don't scare her.

Beat. Beat.

DILPREET: So what you wanting me to do?

JASMEET: Give her a few days to calm down . . . try to make everything normal, and if that doesn't work, we'll go from there. She is not like Mumma, Dad. And now . . . they have meds for these things.

DILPREET: Jassie . . .

JASMEET: Trust me, Dad.

DILPREET sits. Beat. JASMEET gives him a hug.

SCENE 14

A day later. Evening. DILPREET and IYAR are on stage. IYAR looks sharp in his prom suit. DILPREET is really excited. He is holding a camera with a flash.

DILPREET: JASMEET! HURRY, NA!

JASMEET: *(off stage)* COMING!

DILPREET: Aare, hurry na, Jassie! How long you make Tamil teeth wait?

IYAR: It's okay.

DILPREET: You don't know this one. She will take seven hundred years if you don't hurry. You are having money?

IYAR: Yes, Uncle.

DILPREET: You are having cellphone fully charged?

IYAR: Yes, Uncle.

DILPREET: You are having drink tonight?

IYAR almost falls for it.

IYAR: Ye . . . No. I mean, no.

DILPREET yells to JASMEET.

DILPREET: JASSI! Come! Come now!

(to IYAR) You wanting solo shot of you?

IYAR: No, it's okay.

DILPREET: Don't be shy. I am take for you. Move there.

Pause.

No. There.

Pause.

No. Here is best. Okay. Be like model.

IYAR: Sorry, what?

DILPREET: Model. Model. Be like model! Make a pose.

DILPREET demonstrates.

Stand like this. Chest out. Like brave man. Fearless man. Why you today's young man stand like you never drink milk?

IYAR poses.

IYAR: Oh. Okay.

DILPREET: Fantas.

He takes a picture.

Very good.

JASMEET enters with SIMRAN behind her. She looks beautiful in her dress.

OH MY GOD! Jassie! Look at you! Look at your hair!

IYAR: That's my homegirl #1!

JASMEET: I know, right! I really look stunning! It's called a *sock bun.* There is an actual sock in my bun. And you know what's gonna look even more awesome around that bun? My prom queen crown! Seriously. We're gonna own that prom!

SIMRAN's hands are twitching. No one notices but the audience. IYAR pins a corsage on JASMEET. It's a cute moment.

DILPREET: Come on! I am take picture, you two. Come on!

IYAR and JASMEET pose.

All right, smiling everyone. Show teeth. Teeth.

They smile.

(to IYAR) What is wrong with your teeth? So white . . . white like polar bear white. Why they so white?

JASMEET: Dad!

He takes the picture.

Another one for good luck.

IYAR: You look bomb!

JASMEET: I know, right!

He takes another one.

DILPREET: Jassie, I am needing solo of you.

IYAR: We gotto go, J—

JASMEET does a couple of poses. DILPREET takes pictures. A limo honks its horn outside.

JASMEET: Wait! I want one with Simmi and Dad. Iyar, take the camera.

DILPREET: Why you not give me warning. I would wear suit, put some cologne, and polish my shoe.

JASMEET: Come on come on come on. Hurry!

They all pose. IYAR takes a picture. The limo honks again.

Okay. Gotta go. Bye, bye.

DILPREET: Be safe. Jassie, you not / drinking.

JASMEET: Relax, Dad.

IYAR gives the camera back to DILPREET.

IYAR: Thanks, Uncle.

DILPREET: You taking care of this half brain.

IYAR: Don't worry.

They exit. JASMEET runs back in and hugs SIMRAN. In the hug SIMRAN smells her flowers.

JASMEET: Thank you thank you thank you. I love you. We're gonna win this for sure.

JASMEET exits.

SIMRAN: She is so so beautiful. She looks just like Mumma. Don't you think she looks just like Mumma?

Beat.

Mumma thinks so.

DILPREET: You wanting something to eat? I am hungry. We have chicken. Spicy chicken with paratha.

DILPREET exits to the kitchen. SIMRAN stands and takes a deep breath in. Beat. She takes another breath in. Beat. And another one. It's almost like she is breathing in every essence of her mother.

SCENE 15

Midnight. SIMRAN enters. She stands for a beat. She walks around. She looks at herself in the store mirrors. She looks for something but can't find it. She looks in the drawers and finds a hand mirror. She looks at herself and sits. She is staring at her reflection. She makes exaggerated/distorted faces at the mirror.

The following is not distressing. She is being specific. As if reading a grocery list.

SIMRAN: My name is Simran Singh. Dad's name is Dilpreet Singh. Jassie is my sister. S-I-M-R-A-N S-I-N-G-H. 2424 Gerrard Street. Toronto. Ontario. M4E 2E9. S-I-M-R-A-N S-I-N-G-H S-I-M-R-A-N S-I-N-G-H. 2424 Gerrard Street. Toronto. Ontario. M4E 2E9. S-I-M-R-A-N S-I-N-G-H.

SIMRAN continues to make exaggerated faces at the mirror. Beat. She throws the mirror. It doesn't break. Beat. She picks it up and puts it back in its place. She exits.

SCENE 16

JASMEET is on stage with a prom queen crown on her head arranging for a family meeting. She is ringing the family meeting bell as she speaks loudly, calling on DILPREET and SIMRAN off stage.

JASMEET: *(calling)* All right all right all right, where is everybody? Why is everyone late now?! Come on, people, we have just four more days till opening!

She rings the bell a couple more times.

Hello! Hello! Hello! Family meeting time!

SIMRAN enters from outside.

Hello, what the hell? Where've you been?

SIMRAN: Sorry.

JASMEET: Come on, Dad. Simmi is back.

DILPREET enters from the back room with a massive box of parandis. He notices JASMEET's prom queen crown.

DILPREET: It be three days, why you still wear that stupid thing on your head?

JASMEET: *(practical)* Because it enhances my cheekbones.

(re: parandis) Please leave them for now, I'll do it later. Okay, so, I am chairing this meeting—

DILPREET: What chair? There is no chair. I am boss. I am have agenda—

JASMEET: I know, but I would like to propose a change, so I am chairing—

DILPREET: Jassie, close your mouth. Simmi, do minute.

He hands the minutes book to SIMRAN. SIMRAN, *disinterested and restless, tries to focus and take notes.*

Okay, item number one on the agenda: opening day gift boxes. Item number two: delegations of responsibilities—

JASMEET: Delegating—

DILPREET: What I am say to you about your mouth? Item number three: What the status of the reesveeps on the inviting list?

SIMRAN: What?

DILPREET: What, what? The reesveeps.

JASMEET: *(to SIMRAN)* RSVPS.

(to DILPREET) Keep going.

DILPREET: Item one. Thank-you box. Okay, so, I am talk to Sukhvindar Singh Ji at BJ Supermarket and he is saying that he think the top-notch number-one idea be that when a customer come in on Canada Day opening day and just walk around the store and just *look* we to give them a thank-you box that have one samosa and two laddoo. BUT the moment a customer *buying* something from us on Canada Day opening day, we to give them bigger box with two samosa and two laddoo—

JASMEET: Okay, no, stop, Dad, that's just stupid—

DILPREET: Why stupid? That way we showing *more* appreciate to customer who spend money—

JASMEET: First of all, two sets of boxes will be WAY too confusing—

DILPREET: But one will be bigger box—

JASMEET: Secondly, do you really want people to find out that some people have less and some people have more in the boxes? They are Indians. They're gonna start fighting over who has more. I vote NO. Simmi?

SIMRAN: *(disinterested)* No.

DILPREET realizes JASMEET is right.

DILPREET: Jassie, you *do* have brain inside that empty head. I am impress.

JASMEET: I'm glad you noticed. Okay, so, here is my—

DILPREET: Waiting. I am not finish. So, now, with only one box on this discussion, should we be doing two samosa and two laddoo OR because samosa is more popular among the Canada people, we do three samosa and one laddoo—

JASMEET: OR how about my idea where we don't do either—

DILPREET: No box?

JASMEET: *(selling)* No no no . . . of course we're gonna do a thank-you box—of course—BUT how about we jazz it up. Do something different. Do something exciting. We'll give South Indian delicacies. Like vada and idli from the amazing Castle Nadu—

DILPREET: Is Tamil teeth that desperate in need of money—

JASMEET: No, Dad, don't be ridiculous. I just think it's such a great idea. AND I spoke with Iyar's uncle and he said if we order from them he will give us a ten percent discount.

DILPREET: Ooooooohhh! Ten percent, I am buying my own castle with that—

JASMEET: That's more than BJS is giving. I am calling the question. It's time to vote. I vote YES, Simmi. Please. Castle Nadu's food is amazing. Vote yes—

SIMRAN: Yes—

DILPREET: I am veto. I am think three samosa and one laddoo—

JASMEET: Dad! You can't veto!

DILPREET: Of course I am veto. I am boss!

JASMEET: Dad!

DILPREET: Veto veto veto.

JASMEET: Fine, but your box will be crap. Do two and two. Make it equal at least.

DILPREET: Okay, equal. I am vote YES.

SIMRAN: Yes.

DILPREET: Good. Done. Next. Now, delegations of responsibilities. On the day, Jassie I am need you to be on cash taking money and drawing receipts as I am doing packing. Simmi, I am need you to be on floor greeting, talking.

SIMRAN: I won't do it—

DILPREET: It is the best plan—

SIMRAN: No.

DILPREET: Why? What you wanting then—

SIMRAN: I don't want to meet new people—

DILPREET: Simmi—

JASMEET: Don't force her, Dad. She can do cash. I'm not good with numbers. We'll swap. I'll talk and greet.

JASMEET winks at SIMRAN.

Moving on. Item three. RSVPs. So far we've had about 160 YES, a couple of MAYBES and about fifty or fifty-five NO. So, because of the number of NOs I think we can invite some random people. I can invite some of Iyar's mom's friends. They're rich—they have money. Simmi can invite work people from the library, and if you want, Dad, we could also invite—

SIMRAN: No one from the library will come.

JASMEET: Why? They love you there.

SIMRAN: Not anymore.

JASMEET: What do you mean?

SIMRAN: I quit.

JASMEET: What?

DILPREET: What you mean quit?

SIMRAN: I quit working there.

DILPREET: Quit, quit?

JASMEET: When did you do that—

SIMRAN: A while ago—

DILPREET: What? So where you go when you go to work—

JASMEET: Why did you do that—

Pause.

Simmi—

SIMRAN: This meeting is adjourned.

JASMEET: No it's not. Answer the question.

SIMRAN: It's none of your goddamn business.

JASMEET: What do you mean it's none of my goddamn business? You're my sister, so it *is* my—

SIMRAN: *(calmly)* Fuck you.

Beat.

JASMEET is completely taken aback.

JASMEET: What?

SIMRAN: *(calmly)* Fuck. You.

JASMEET: Wait. What's happening right now—

DILPREET: Simran, watch your mouth—

JASMEET: What the hell is your problem—

SIMRAN is calm. She says the following "Fuck you" speech almost in a sing-song voice. She keeps going under DILPREET and JASMEET's lines until "What the hell is wrong with you."

SIMRAN: Fuck you. Fuck you. Fuck you. Fuck you. / Fuck you. And you and you and you and you. Fuck you. Fuck you.

DILPREET: Simran, I am say watch your mouth—

JASMEET: Stop it. Stop. What the hell is wrong with you?

SIMRAN: *(calmly)* I don't have to answer your goddamn questions. I don't have to answer anyone's goddamn questions about where I go, what I do, who I see, who I am with, why I am late, what I drink, what I want, and why and why and why and why and why. I want to do what I want to do. Okay, Jasmeet. Okay, Dad. I just want to do what I want to do.

(calmly, sing-song) Fuck you. Fuck you. Fuck you. Fuck you—

JASMEET: You're an asshole.

JASMEET exits, slamming the door. DILPREET sits. SIMRAN sits.

SCENE 17

The next day. JASMEET *and* IYAR *are sitting together with the shipment box of parandis open beside them. They are braiding and colour-coordinating them.*

JASMEET: Do it properly, Iyar!

IYAR: I am! It's a perfect braid.

JASMEET: It's crooked. Either do it right or don't do it at all.

IYAR: It looks fine! Look at it. It looks fine!

IYAR *looks at her. Smiles.*

JASMEET: What?

IYAR: I have a surprise for you.

JASMEET: Not now, Iyar—

IYAR: You'll love it. I swear—

JASMEET: Not now, please! We have to finish these so Dad doesn't freak about them being disorganized—

IYAR *pulls out a stack of prom pictures.* JASMEET *breaks out into a huge smile.*

IYAR! Let me see let me see!

IYAR: What did I say!?

JASMEET: Show show show me!

She rips open the envelope and starts to look through them.

When did you print them! These are amazing! Oh my God! We look amazing. This one, okay, I'm getting it framed. This is like a prom classic. Look at it! And look at this one. My chin is perfectly angled! Man, I look good on that stage. Look at the crown! And can I just say we look like a *power couple.*

IYAR: What are those?

JASMEET: Power couple— Like the couples who own the world. You know? Like Zendaya and Tom. Clooney and that lawyer lady. Like, they are the shit and they know it.

Pause. Analyzing.

I am legit like so pretty. I look like Dipika. Actually, no, I don't look that Bollywood. I look like a sexy cross between Kendall and Kylie. Now that's rare.

IYAR: You did have a lot of makeup on.

JASMEET: Shut up!

They kiss.

Wow. Look at this. I love this. We look so cute.

IYAR: You look cute.

JASMEET: I know!

They look through more pictures. IYAR cuddles her. SIMRAN has entered but neither JASMEET nor IYAR can see her. Visible to the audience, she hides behind the doorway looking at both of them.

You looked hot in that.

IYAR: Oh ya?

JASMEET: Ya.

IYAR: How hot?

JASMEET: Smokin' hot.

IYAR: Like *really really* smokin' or *just a little* smokin' hot?

JASMEET: Like *holy fuck I wanna rip your shirt off* smokin' hot!

They giggle and kiss. IYAR *goes in for a deep kiss.*

Okay, stop stop stop. We have to finish these. How 'bout this, we finish these and then go see a movie and we can make out at the theatre.

IYAR: But your dad said we had to be here in case Simran needed anything.

JASMEET: We've been here all morning. She doesn't need anything. She's fine. I wanna go. So hurry up so we can get popcorn.

IYAR: J, I honestly don't think we should. We should be here in case—

JASMEET: She is *my* sister, Iyar. I read on this psychology blog the more you pay attention to stress and anxiety the bigger it gets. There's no need for us to babysit her.

IYAR: It's not, babe, it's way more than that!

JASMEET: I know her. She is always like this—

IYAR: Always like what? J, she ran away. People just don't do that! This is big shit. I told you she sounds manic—

JASMEET: Stop it—

IYAR: Don't do one of those weird denial things—

JASMEET: I am in denial? I'm the one screaming at Dad that she needs some space. Everyone needs to chill out and let her have some time—

IYAR: J, when you have to report someone missing, they don't need time, they need help!

JASMEET: I *am* helping, Iyar. What else am I supposed to do? What the fuck do you think we're doing right now? I do every fucking thing for this store so she can manage her shit. I organized the entire opening invites, I called the wholesale suppliers, I picked the patterns of the lehengas, I picked the signboard colour, I did the flyer design, and on and on and on. All of it I did. I can tell you how much each and every thing costs in this fucking store. And you know why? Because I know how much my dad needs this.

And for the last two weeks all I have done is read about this anxiety crap online. Every single fucking night I am on some goddamn psych blog or forum trying to figure out what the fuck is making her so stressed.

And she has gotten headaches all her life, by the way. It's *nothing* new. She gets a headache, Dad panics. She needs the lights dimmed, Dad panics. She is anxious, Dad panics. That's what he does. You see how he is about us. It's how it works in this family.

Fuck.

IYAR hugs JASMEET. He kisses her. It's a beautiful, compassionate moment. He holds her. They kiss again. As they kiss SIMRAN touches her crotch. The more passionately they kiss the more she presses her crotch. SIMRAN exits. JASMEET is suddenly aware of movement. She pulls away.

What was that?

IYAR: What?

JASMEET speaks towards the door.

JASMEET: Hello?

IYAR: No one's there.

JASMEET: I swear I heard something . . . Hello?

Pause.

Simmi?

IYAR: Babe, no one's there.

Pause.

JASMEET: *(louder)* Simmi? Are you there?

Pause.

Simmi?

SIMRAN: *(off stage)* What?

JASMEET: What do you need?

SIMRAN: *(off stage)* Nothing.

Pause. SIMRAN *enters. She has taken off all her clothes and is just wearing* DILPREET'S *suit jacket.*

JASMEET: What are you . . . where are your pants?

SIMRAN: I don't know.

JASMEET: What? Why are you wearing that?

SIMRAN: I don't know.

JASMEET: What—

SIMRAN: I don't know.

JASMEET: Go get dressed and get your fucking clothes on.

SIMRAN: I don't know.

JASMEET: Just do it.

An awkward moment as SIMRAN *just stands there.*

Simmi! Why are you just fucking standing there like a zombie. Go.

SIMRAN: *(to* IYAR*)* Why are you here again?

JASMEET: What the fuck is wrong with you?

IYAR: I'm Iyar. We've met, remember? You know me.

SIMRAN: I *know* who you are. Why are you *here*? Are you watching us?

JASMEET: Are you kidding me? Are you fucking stupid?

SIMRAN: Are you *watching* us?

JASMEET: Whatever this shit you're doing, it's done. I want you to drop it right now.

SIMRAN: What?

JASMEET: I am serious. Drop it.

SIMRAN: I *know* you are watching us.

IYAR: Simran, we met last week, remember?

JASMEET: What? What the fuck what the fuck what the fuck are you doing? Seriously! You keep this shit up, Dad is gonna throw you in some fucking shithole and you'll be gone. Is that what you want? If so, keep it up. Seriously. Keep it up.

SIMRAN: Where is she?

JASMEET: Who?

SIMRAN is suspicious, aggressive.

SIMRAN: Where IS she?

JASMEET: *(realization)* Wait wait wait wait . . . just realized now what the fuck you've been doing. I know *exactly* what the fuck you've been doing. This is all fucking bullshit. You're just trying to get out of law school. This is your way of getting out of it. You're scared you won't get the grade. Because you know you won't cut it—

SIMRAN repeatedly raises an arm and brings it down to her ear.

What the fuck are you doing now?

IYAR: J, please—

JASMEET: STOP IT! SIMMI! / Stop!

IYAR: Stop yelling! You're making it worse!

SIMRAN: Does she. Do you . . . Does she.

JASMEET: What?

SIMRAN: Do you talk? To her?

JASMEET: What?

SIMRAN: Mumma, does she talk to you? Do you talk with her?

JASMEET: Oh my God, be normal, damn it!

IYAR: Simran, who are you talking about?

SIMRAN: Not loudly. Just whispers—

JASMEET: SHUT UP, SIMRAN! BE NORMAL—

IYAR: You're making it worse, J! Stop it!

SIMRAN: *(to IYAR)* Can you hear her right now—

JASMEET: What—

SIMRAN: I can hear her right now. Is she coming?

JASMEET: Simran—

SIMRAN: Wait wait, she is listening. Right there. Right there. Right there. Can you hear? Can you, Jassie? Do you? Hear it?

JASMEET: Shit. Shit. Shit. Shit. Shit. Shit . . .

SIMRAN: Yes yes yes yes yes yes yes . . . Mumma said . . . Mumma said . . . Mumma said . . . Mumma said—

SIMRAN stands up on the table. Suddenly she is terrified. SIMRAN can see her dead mother hanging. She screams . . .

MUMMA NO!

DILPREET enters. SIMRAN is panicking. She repeats "MUMMA NO" though DILPREET and JASMEET's dialogue.

DILPREET: *(overlapping)* Simmi? Why you are standing there?

JASMEET: *(overlapping)* What the fuck are you doing—

IYAR: *(overlapping)* Simran!

DILPREET: *(overlapping)* Why are . . . Where are your clothes? Cover yourself, Simmi!

JASMEET: *(overlapping)* Simmi, come down—

DILPREET: *(overlapping)* Get her something . . . get down—

JASMEET: *(overlapping)* Dad! Come down, Simmi.

IYAR: *(overlapping)* Simran! Please, Jasmeet!

SIMRAN panics. She doesn't want to come down.

SIMRAN: *(overlapping)* NO! GET AWAY . . . GET AWAY FROM ME, MUMMA! YOU'RE SCARING ME!

JASMEET: We're here. Right here.

DILPREET: *(overlapping)* Simmi! Stop . . . Simmi!

SIMRAN: *(overlapping)* Get away. Where . . . no! No! No!

IYAR: Jassie, leave her!

DILPREET: SIMMI! WHAT YOU ARE—

JASMEET: Simmi, please. Calm down—

SIMRAN: GET AWAY FROM ME!

JASMEET: What the hell!?

SIMRAN: *(fast)* GET THE FUCK AWAY FROM ME! NO. NO. NO. GO AWAY, MUMMA, PLEASE. I DON'T WANNA SEE YOUR FACE. YOU'RE SCARING ME, PLEASE! NO. NO. NO. NO. PLEASE. PLEASE, MUMMA. MUMMA. MUMMA. GO AWAY! GO AWAY! YOU'RE SCARING ME! MUMMA!

DILPREET: It's okay, Simmi. It's . . . Mumma is gone now. It's okay.

DILPREET repeats this until SIMRAN calms down.

SIMRAN's mood switches. SIMRAN sees her mother appear and she is happy to see her.

SIMRAN: Red. Red sari. Yellow border. Golden trim. The old house. The backyard. The tree.

DILPREET: I know . . . I know, Buubbla. I know.

SIMRAN is elated with this memory. None of it is painful. It is pure joy.

SIMRAN: *(quickly)* She is . . . swaying. You . . . you remember, Dad. She is swaying. She just keeps going back and forth. I am—I don't. I am watching. You remember, Dad? I am watching from the window and I see her. I see so I go to the old backyard. She looks perfect. She has just bathed. Her hair is parted. Bindi in place. She she smells of fresh talcum powder. I watch her sway, Dad. From the tree. You remember? Swaying back and forth. You are you are arranging receipts. I take your hand and you laugh. I lead you to the the the the the the the the the window.

Jhankar. Jhankar. Jhankar.

Beat.

Again and again and again and again you screamed Mumma's name. Remember, Dad? We go to the backyard together.

Beat.

I am watching you screaming again. I can't hear anything. Your face is red. I vomit now. Vomit on my lap. When did I sit down? Last night's roti. Roti, chicken curry, and rajma. You are trying to undo the knot around Mumma's neck. It's on tight. Mumma's face looks ugly. I realize I have a really ugly mother.

I watch you yank her down. Onto the grass. I look at her. She is . . . still so ugly. How did I have such an ugly mother? I have to tell Jassie this. She needs to know that we have an ugly mother.

Where is Jassie? I need to . . . I need to tell her that our mumma is ugly. I need to tell her. Jassie? Jassie? Where is Jassie?

JASMEET: Simmi. I am—

SIMRAN: JASMEET?

JASMEET: Simmi. I'm right here.

SIMRAN: Jassie.

SIMRAN notices JASMEET for the first time.

Jassie?

JASMEET: Simmi, yes. I am here—

SIMRAN: You know . . . you know that Mumma is ugly, right?

JASMEET: Simmi—

SIMRAN: You know this. Right?

Beat.

You know this, right? Right, Jassie? She is. She is really ugly. I saw it. I saw it myself.

Beat.

JASMEET: I know.

SIMRAN: You know?

JASMEET: I know. You told me. Remember?

SIMRAN: I did?

JASMEET: Yes. You told me that night.

SIMRAN: *(relieved)* Good. So, you know.

SIMRAN comes down from the table. JASMEET sits in front of SIMRAN and looks her right in the eye.

JASMEET: *(to SIMRAN)* We are going to go to the emergency room now, okay? All of us.

Okay?

SCENE 18

The next day. Noon. DILPREET is on stage making cardboard boxes. Empty boxes everywhere have "Ranmeet Fusions" stamped on them. JASMEET enters.

JASMEET: Dad, it's almost noon. Why didn't you wake me?

DILPREET: We come back so late last night from hospital, I am not wanting to wake you. You wanting food? I am make you eggs.

JASMEET: Did they call? Did you check in about Simmi this morning?

DILPREET: No—

JASMEET: Why not?

DILPREET: Sukhvindar Singh Ji at BJ Supermarket come by today morning. See see, he specially get them made for us. Ranmeet Fusion stamp and everything. I am say to him that he need help, that you and I do it fast fast and get all these to him by evening time.

JASMEET doesn't react to any of this.

What?

JASMEET: Nothing.

Beat.

It's weird that you're doing this bullshit while Simmi is sitting in some random hospital room scared to death.

DILPREET: What you're wanting me to do? We opening in two days.

JASMEET: Last night while we were waiting in the hospital I was thinking . . . and I think it's a really good idea given the circumstances. I think we should delay the opening.

DILPREET: Where is your brain?

JASMEET: Just listen to me. I think I've got it worked out. I'll send out emails cancelling the RSVPs and I'll personally call the people who don't have email. We don't know what kinda shape she'll be in, Dad, so we can put all the shipment orders on hold. I'll cancel the food, it's not a big deal! We'll open when she is better—

DILPREET: And what if she never get better?

JASMEET: Why would you say that?

DILPREET: What then?

JASMEET: Listen to me. We *have to* postpone the opening—

DILPREET: Use your head for once—

JASMEET: But this is the stupidest thing! She goes in some clinical bullshit mental care room and you are here working away to open the fucking store!

DILPREET goes to a drawer that's previously not been opened by anyone on stage. He pulls out a file folder. As he speaks the following he pulls out papers one by one to support his point.

DILPREET pulls out paper:

DILPREET: Twelve thousand on the shipment for arm and leg bracelet.

Pulls out paper:

Six thousand on decoration shipment.

Pulls out paper:

Twenty-six thousand on the lehenga and parandi and chunni from India.

Pulls out paper:

Seventeen thousand on the silk saris.

Pulls out paper:

Three thousand five hundred on mannequin.

Pulls out paper:

Sixteen thousand on a new roof. On top of this, mortgage, electric, food, your daily spending. And now with Simmi, the money, the medicine, the back forth with doctors, hospital, doctor. How much they all add up to? Ha? How much? You pay?

JASMEET: She is sick, Dad. Seriously sick—

DILPREET: You think I am not know that?! And she get even worse because you, you brainless idiot. How many times I am say she is going mental case? She could have been in the hospital weeks ago. But no no no, "She not like Mumma, Dad. She not like her." And now see. You happy now? She could have kill herself and that would be on your head. We are opening store and that is final!

JASMEET: To open your fucking store you'd abandon your own daughter—

DILPREET: What you say?

JASMEET: It's true.

DILPREET: Say again?

JASMEET: I said "abandon."

DILPREET: Abandon? How these words are coming out of your mouth? You even hearing yourself? I am abandon?

He starts to make boxes. He stops.

(unsentimental) I am never abandon nobody. I am stay. I am work work work for you, for Simmi, for Mumma. Slave for you three. To put hot food in front of your mouth. To keeping slippers on your feet. I am always stay. I am stay here and I am be here for you two even when . . . And now, and now you are twisting around and making me abandon. What you have done? Ha? What you have done for this family? Tell me. No no, I want to hear. Tell me. I am plead bank loan for us. I am touch Patel's feet for money. I am steal milk from the grocery. I am I am go to airport every night and push empty luggage carts to collect quarters so I am able to feed you all. You have done *any* of that? Don't you be telling me that I am abandon. I am I be here. I am right here. Always.

JASMEET: Dad.

DILPREET: Nothing.

JASMEET: Fuck.

DILPREET: Make the boxes. Come on.

DILPREET starts to make boxes. JASMEET stands for a beat. She joins him.

SCENE 19

Four hours later. No one is on stage. There are unopened Chinese food takeout containers on the table. A slight moment. JASMEET enters. She is holding bags.

Excited, IYAR enters from the kitchen. He is holding plates and cutlery.

IYAR: BABY GIRL!

JASMEET: *(screams)* Holy fuck! You scared the shit out of me!

IYAR: What up! What up!

JASMEET: What are you doing here? How'd you get in?

IYAR leans in for a kiss. No dice.

No, seriously, how did you get in?

IYAR: I called like a million times. You're phone was off—

JASMEET: My phones dead. How'd you get in—

IYAR: I came over and your dad said you were out somewhere. Said he tried to call you to let you know . . . but anyway, he is at the hospital—

JASMEET: What? What happened now—

IYAR: Not an emergency, but the doctors at the hospital asked him to come over. The other doctor guy . . . Saleem or something, has gone to meet him there. So, I asked him if I could stay and get us some Chinese food so we could have a late *romantical* lunch together. And he said yes—and walla walla—Chinese and me!

She doesn't respond.

JASMEET: When did he leave?

IYAR: I don't know . . . an hour ago.

JASMEET: So you've been in my house for the last hour.

IYAR: Yes, and I'm starving. Let's eat and then I'll help you decorate for the opening.

Pause.

What?

JASMEET: You know this, don't be stupid, I don't eat Chinese—

IYAR: When did that happen?

JASMEET: Always. You know this—

IYAR: No, I didn't know that. We eat it all the time—

JASMEET: When? When was the last time you and I ate Chinese food?

IYAR: Always—

JASMEET: When?

IYAR: Babe—

JASMEET: No, when?

IYAR: I don't know, like last month . . . We had your favourite chicken ball thingy—

JASMEET: Really? When last month? Tell me *exactly* when—

Pause.

IYAR: Last month . . . like after Roop's party. It was a Friday night . . . I think . . . ya, it was Friday. I had my dad's car. We all went to Mr. Wong's.

Beat.

JASMEET: Right, well, I stopped eating it on the Saturday then.

A long pause. IYAR *is trying to be casual.*

IYAR: What's in that bag?

Pause.

JASMEET: New bedsheets for when Simmi comes home.

IYAR: That'll be a nice surprise.

He pulls out ivory-coloured bedsheets.

They're beautiful. Oh wow. Feel them! Good job, babe.

Notices the price.

Wait, holy fuck, are you shitting me? You spent five hundred and sixty dollars on these things?

JASMEET: What's that supposed to mean?

IYAR: That an insane amount of money for bedsheets. Who does that?

JASMEET: I do. For my sister.

IYAR: You're shitting me.

JASMEET: Oh, so now you're judging us?

IYAR: No . . . I've just . . . never seen that. That's . . . wow. Okay.

Pause.

When do you think she will be able to come home?

JASMEET: How the fuck should I know? Do I look like a doctor?

IYAR: What the fuck, Jasmeet?

JASMEET: Don't do that—

IYAR: Do what? I am just trying to . . . to be here for you.

JASMEET: Trying to be here for me? No, you don't get to be here, in my house, and find out things before I do. Don't come over here with food and talk to my dad about my sister and comment on things I buy her! This is not a party! Fuck.

IYAR: *(sharply)* Look, I wasn't . . . I am sorry.

IYAR goes in for a hug. JASMEET pushes him away.

JASMEET: Fuck, don't touch me.

IYAR: You seriously need to chill the fuck out! You're starting to act like a—

JASMEET: What? Say it. Crazy? I am starting to act like a crazy person? Crazy like my sister? Crazy like my mother?

Beat. Beat. Beat.

IYAR: Babe.

DILPREET enters.

JASMEET: Dad, what happened? How is she?

DILPREET: Everything good. She is *complying*. The hospital doctors give her medicine that she is saying yes to taking and Saleem think it's good too.

JASMEET: When's she getting home?

DILPREET: I am signing form tomorrow and bringing her home. So, it's good. That's good. I am having to sign paper to taking care of her. But we have to go back again for more testing in two week.

DILPREET notices the bedsheets.

What's that?

IYAR: Bedsheets. She bought them. For Simran.

DILPREET: Oh, good. Good, Jassie.

JASMEET: Thank you.

(sarcastically) It's expensive though. Hope that's okay around here.

JASMEET exits. Beat.

IYAR: Is Simran going to be okay, Uncle?

DILPREET: Yes, okay, yes, ya, yes.

IYAR: Uncle, you want some Chinese food?

DILPREET: Not this garbage. I make fresh for you. We have to keep going. Come. I'll make for you.

DILPREET exits to make food.

SCENE 20

Same day, evening. DILPREET is packing a small travel bag. He folds SIMRAN's shirt, a pair of pants, underwear, and a bra. He pulls out a new water bottle from a plastic bag, cuts the price tag off, and places the bottle in the travel bag along with a box of laddoos. He zips up the bag and sist. A long pause.

SCENE 21

JASMEET is waiting for SIMRAN. An extended pause. She realizes the lights are too bright for SIMRAN—she dims them. DILPREET and SIMRAN enter. She is wearing the clothes DILPREET packed for her and is holding the red water bottle.

JASMEET: SIMMI! Welcome welcome welcome welcome! Sit sit sit. How're you doing?

SIMRAN: Good. I'm good.

JASMEET: Come. Sit. Here.

SIMRAN sits.

You wanna eat? You're hungry, right?

DILPREET: Of course she hungry!

SIMRAN: Ya, a little bit.

JASMEET: Okay, wait, I'll be right back. Wait. I have amazing Chinese.

JASMEET exits. In the following section, as DILPREET and SIMRAN are left on stage, there is an extended pause where JASMEET can be heard in the kitchen.

Cutlery sounds. The microwave opening. The food being heated. Beeping. JASMEET removing the plate.

JASMEET enters holding a hot pate of Chinese food.

It's not from the shithole down the street, by the way, but from Mr. Wong's. Careful, its hot.

As the scene progresses SIMRAN *keeps picking at the chicken balls.*

So, here is what I'm thinking—

DILPREET: Do it later, no, Jassie—

JASMEET: No. Dad, please. I'm excited. I was thinking, because you're home now and you know . . . in case you wanna spend more time in your bedroom, that, you know, we spruce it up. Give it some class. So, I bought you a little present.

JASMEET brings out a beautifully wrapped present with a huge bow on it.

And, by the way, I bought this with my *own* money. You know, just in case you're wondering. Open it!

SIMRAN opens the package.

BEDSHEETS!

SIMRAN: Oh, wow.

JASMEET: I know, right! Ivory! There are like ten billion varieties of white bedsheets. But this was the best. Right? It's like royal-looking.

DILPREET: Good choice, Jassie!

SIMRAN: They're really nice. I love them. Thank you.

JASMEET: And it's like seven trillion thread count, by the way. Seriously.

She opens the sheets and takes them to SIMRAN.

Feel it.

SIMRAN feels them. She goes back to eating the chicken balls.

Okay, so the other thing, I think, that would be great is if we can paint your room. After the opening tomorrow, we'll paint it. Next weekend. I brought colour samples today, and look—

JASMEET brings out a handful of colour samples.

My favourite is the paradise blue or or or a softer one, water jet blue. What do you think?

She hands the colour samples to SIMRAN.

Here, you pick a colour? Which one do you like?

SIMRAN looks at the colours while she eats.

I can get it tonight.

Beat.

It's not a big deal. We can start next weekend. Now, about tomorrow, we *need* to have a quick family meeting for the opening. So—

DILPREET: We can do this later, no, Jassie?

JASMEET: Later when? We open *tomorrow*, Dad.

She gets the family meeting bell.

There is no later. Later is now.

She rings the bell.

We don't need to do minutes 'cause it's a quick one. Let's do this. Okay, so, what's the status with BJ?

DILPREET: All good. They say they will have everything ready for picking up for 9:30 tomorrow morning.

JASMEET: That's late. That's way too late.

DILPREET: These are Indian's, Jassie, no one running on time.

JASMEET: Okay, but you better make sure they are here BEFORE we open. And Iyar will be here to help. So take him with you.

DILPREET: Okay, okay.

She rings the bell.

JASMEET: Delegations review. Okay. So, as previously decided, I am greeting people. Simmi is on cash. Dad, you're selling. And Iyar is gonna hand out gift boxes.

Yes. Okay. Good. Now, last point. In good news, we have about twenty more "yes" RSVPS.

DILPREET: That is fantas, Jassie! And I am sure we have a lot walks-ins coming too.

JASMEET: And and and guess who said they are coming for sure!!

(to SIMRAN) Amar! Roop's hot cousin. The guy who likes you, remember?

DILPREET: Good. That's good. Tell Amar there is free laddoo, no? He bring more friends. Okay, so we adjourn meeting—

SIMRAN: Can you invite Doctor Saleem? I want him to come.

DILPREET: Yes. For sure. Okay. Yes. I am go call him. I am go call him right now. This is good.

SIMRAN gags.

What happen?

SIMRAN: I have to puke.

SIMRAN exits.

DILPREET: Why you give her so much Chinese food? Now look what you do!

DILPREET goes after SIMRAN.

Simran!

JASMEET: I was just trying to help.

DILPREET exits. JASMEET just sits there. Not sure what else to do.

SCENE 22

Hours later. Middle of the night. SIMRAN sits by herself. She has the ivory bedsheets wrapped around her. She is looking out.

DILPREET enters. He sits beside SIMRAN.

DILPREET: You happy, na?

Pause.

You happy, Buubbla?

SIMRAN: I am so sorry.

Beat. They both just sit.

SIMRAN gets up and as she leaves she touches DILPREET's hand.

SIMRAN exits, DILPREET sits. He looks at the lines on his palms.

DILPREET: The lines say that we are to do this together, you and me, Jhankar, you and me. We are to do this together. The lines in my hand are like the same lines in your hand, remember?

Beat.

All this we dream. Together. All this. Remember, Jhankar? This not just me. This me and you. We dream together . . .

Unbeknownst to DILPREET, SIMRAN re-enters.

When Simmi born, you say to me, you say, "This be our golden child," our golden child . . .

But now my *golden child*, she disappearing.

Beat.

Her face be grey, her eyes they hollow, her teeth they don't smile anymore. She caught between me and where you be.

She walking to you.

Beat.

Turn her back to me. Turn her back to me.

Beat.

Jhankar, turn back our *golden child* . . . turn her back to me.

DILPREET senses something. He turns around. DILPREET and SIMRAN look at each other. An extended pause.

SCENE 23

Opening day. The store is decorated with lots of Canada Day decorations. It looks bright and colourful. JASMEET enters dressed in traditional Indian clothing. It's almost 10 a.m.

JASMEET: Come on come on come on! Fifteen minutes left till the doors open! Come on, Simmi. Let's go!

IYAR and DILPREET enter from the main entrance with gift boxes filled with sweets.

You guys! Hurry up!

IYAR: Babe, help us with these—

JASMEET: Okay, my part of decorating is done and now you guys are running late. What did I tell you. Didn't I say this was gonna happen?

DILPREET: Close your mouth and open hands—

JASMEET: Okay, but didn't I say this was gonna—

DILPREET: Yes, yes, but BJ market boys running late. What I am to do? But, here, smell smell, smell the boxes. It smell so fresh, no?

He smells a box.

Total fantas! Where Simmi be?

JASMEET: *(to DILPREET)* She's getting dressed.

(to SIMRAN) HURRY, SIMMI! We're ready!

DILPREET: She takc her morning pills.

JASMEET: I made sure she did—

DILPREET: Check pill box. Ask her—

JASMEET: I put them in her mouth with my own hands. I know what Saleem said.

DILPREET: Jassie—

JASMEET: I'm on it—

SIMRAN enters. She is wearing a beautiful Indian outfit.

DILPREET: Ohh! Look who is looking fantas today! You are looking good today, Simmi!

SIMRAN: Ya. Jassie did a good job. Yes.

JASMEET: Look how killer her hairstyle is. I did it myself!

IYAR: *(to SIMRAN)* Lookin' good, good lookin'!

DILPREET: Just total fantas! Total fantas!

SIMRAN: It's nice.

DILPREET: Okay, so we are almost good to go. Yes, Jassie?

SIMRAN: Where's my red water bottle?

JASMEET: What?

SIMRAN: My red water bottle.

IYAR hands her the red water bottle.

IYAR: It got moved when we were organizing. Here you go.

SIMRAN chugs the entire bottle.

SIMRAN: I need some more.

SIMRAN exits to get some water.

DILPREET: That is number four she is drinking from today morning.

JASMEET: *(to DILPREET)* Relax. Remember, Saleem said it's just the side effects. She'll be thirsty a lot.

DILPREET: *(looking around)* Where the LSIT books I am arrange already?

JASMEET: I moved them, Dad. It's too much!

DILPREET: Put it back. Where you move them . . . put it back.

JASMEET: No, please, Dad. Normalize it!

DILPREET: Just do it. That *will* make her full normal—

IYAR brings out SIMRAN's law books that JASMEET had moved.

Good. See, this is good boy.

SIMRAN re-enters.

SIMRAN: I want to change the order. I want to be the greeter.

DILPREET: No no, you do the numbers that you wanted. Jassie do greeting. Cash is good, Simmi.

SIMRAN: I want to greet.

Beat.

I can.

(to JASMEET) Is that okay?

JASMEET: Of course, ya.

(lightly) I have a calculator. I'll be fine.

SIMRAN opens one of the gift boxes filled with sweets. No one is sure what to say.

SIMRAN: Happy birthday to Ranmeet! Happy birthday to Ranmeet, happy birthday Ranmeet Fusions, happy birthday to Ranmeet!

DILPREET: Fantas, Simmi! Fantas first birthday, Ranmeet!

JASMEET: First one is for the family and we need to celebrate!

They all share the sweets from the gift box. SIMRAN starts picking at her laddoo.

JASMEET checks the time.

Okay, we ready?

IYAR: Here we go!

DILPREET: Ready, Simmi? Everybody ready?

There's general excitement shared among all of them.

JASMEET: Let's go let's go let's go. Five. Four. Three. Two. One!

DILPREET: Turn on music. Turn on. GO!

JASMEET turns on the music. "Oh, Canada" blasts through the speakers.

JASMEET: Iyar, take the sidewalk sign out and make sure you chain it to the pole so fat boy doesn't steal it.

IYAR exits with the sign.

DILPREET: Good good good, and now we begin.

JASMEET and DILPREET open the main doors. They both step outside to wait for people to come in. As "Oh, Canada" continues to play SIMRAN walks towards the main entrance. She stands for a beat. She wants to do this. She stands for a long pause.

She is determined to do it.

Music and lights snap out.

The end.

ACKNOWLEDGEMENTS

I would like to offer my sincere thanks to Dr. Eilenna Denisoff, Iris Turcott, Nina Lee Aquino, Factory Theatre, Matt McGeachy, the incredible cast—Sugith, Farah, Shruti, and Shelly—the creative team, Dr. Steven Cohen, Ian Arnold, Rena Zimmerman, Playwrights Canada Press, the Playwrights Guild of Canada, the Canada Council for the Arts, the Ontario Arts Council, the Toronto Arts Council, Cahoots Theatre, Studio 180 Theatre, Barbara Laing, Zorana Sadiq, Joanna Barrotta, Thomas Morgan Jones, Hina Khan, and my incredible family: Ma, Baba, Di, Peter, and Aakashie. A special thank you to my husband, Ryan—thank you for being my beloved.

Anusree is a Governor General's Literary Award–nominated and four time Dora Mavor Moore Award–winning writer and actor. For theatre, Anusree's plays include *Through the Eyes of God*, *Trident Moon*, *Little Pretty and The Exceptional*, *Sultans of the Street*, *Brothel #9*, *Roshni*, *Letters to my Grandma*, and *Pyaasa*. She is the recipient of the K.M. Hunter Artist Award, the RBC Emerging Artist Award, the Carol Bolt Award, and the Siminovitch Protégé Prize. She was a 2018 finalist for the Susan Smith Blackburn Prize (the largest and oldest playwriting prize for women writing for English-speaking theatre). She is also an adjunct professor of playwriting at the University of Toronto and a professor of creative writing, teaching advanced drama to M.F.A. students at the University of British Columbia.